"My friend Anita's 'think-out-lou ... h
giggles and truth, reminding me h... .... s!
I don't want to miss another day of technicolor living!"

—VIRELLE KIDDER, conference speaker; author, *Donkeys Still Talk*

"Look up funny in the dictionary and you will find Anita Renfroe.
Whenever Anita takes the platform, the gospel is communicated
in technicolor."

—KATHY TROCCOLI, author, speaker, recording artist

"Beware: you should not read this book while eating or you might
choke from the inevitable giggle-fest."

—ELLIE KAY, international speaker; author, *The Debt Diet*

"Open her book! Read, laugh, inhale, and exhale the great love of
God for His girls and the contents of their purses—good, bad,
messy, and sacred."

—BONNIE KEEN, founding member of First Call,
author, recording artist, speaker

"All too often, Christians are perceived as stiff, formal and humor-
less, but Anita Renfroe blows that stereotype right out of the water!
She has the unique gift of getting people to 'uncross their arms'
through her zany wit and then impacting their hearts through
biblical truth."

—LISA HARPER, author, *Every Woman's Hope* and *Relentless Love*

"The problem with this book is it's just too darn funny! You'll be
laughing so hard that you'll be likely to miss Anita's profound and
hilarious insights on daily life, marriage, and family. Don't get less
than two copies—you'll need more!"

—C. MCNAIR WILSON, speaker; churchgoer;
author, *Raised in Captivity*

the purse-driven life

It really is all about me

Anita Renfroe

NAVPRESS®

BRINGING TRUTH TO LIFE

OUR GUARANTEE TO YOU

We believe so strongly in the message of our books that we are making this quality guarantee to you. If for any reason you are disappointed with the content of this book, return the title page to us with your name and address and we will refund to you the list price of the book. To help us serve you better, please briefly describe why you were disappointed. Mail your refund request to: NavPress, P.O. Box 35002, Colorado Springs, CO 80935.

The Navigators is an international Christian organization. Our mission is to reach, disciple, and equip people to know Christ and to make Him known through successive generations. We envision multitudes of diverse people in the United States and every other nation who have a passionate love for Christ, live a lifestyle of sharing Christ's love, and multiply spiritual laborers among those without Christ.

NavPress is the publishing ministry of The Navigators. NavPress publications help believers learn biblical truth and apply what they learn to their lives and ministries. Our mission is to stimulate spiritual formation among our readers.

ISBN 1-57683-605-3

Cover design by Brand Navigation
Cover photo by Don Jones Photography LLC
Makeup Artist/Stylist: Sue Cary Mayer
Creative Team: Terry Behimer, Arvid Wallen, Traci Mullins, Cara Iverson, Pat Miller

Some of the anecdotal illustrations in this book are true to life and are included with the permission of the persons involved. All other illustrations are composites of real situations, and any resemblance to people living or dead is coincidental.

Unless otherwise identified, all Scripture quotations in this publication are taken from the HOLY BIBLE: NEW INTERNATIONAL VERSION® (NIV®). Copyright © 1973, 1978, 1984 by International Bible Society. Used by permission of Zondervan Publishing House. All rights reserved. Other versions used include: *THE MESSAGE* (MSG). Copyright © 1993, 1994, 1995, 1996, 2000, 2001, 2002. Used by permission of NavPress Publishing Group; the *Amplified New Testament* (AMP), © The Lockman Foundation 1954, 1958; and the *King James Version* (KJV).

Renfroe, Anita, 1962-
  The purse-driven life : it really is all about me / Anita Renfroe.
    p. cm.
  ISBN 1-57683-605-3
  1. Christian women--Religious life. I. Title.
  BV4527.R46 2005
  248.8'43--dc22
                                    2004020349

Printed in the United States of America

2 3 4 5 6 7 8 9 10 / 09 08 07 06 05

FOR A FREE CATALOG OF NAVPRESS BOOKS & BIBLE STUDIES,
CALL 1-800-366-7788 (USA) OR 1-800-839-4769 (CANADA)

contents

official
disclaimer

Thank you for reading this page. I know that a lot of people buy books just to prove they are literary; they never actually get around to reading them. They do this little "Mobile Book Tour" as they initially fall in love with the *cover* and *idea* of a book, which instigates their purchase. They take their new book to the car and drive it home and completely forget that it is in the backseat. There it languishes in the hot sun and dark nights, buried beneath the McDonald's bags and the pile of stuff to be dropped off at Goodwill the next time they pass by. When the faux bibliophiles discover the book (four days later), they have already experienced a "cooling off period," and now their intense passion for the book has subsided considerably. The book will then make the rounds from the front entryway to the bedside, from the bedside to the reading material tote, from the tote to the bookshelf, and finally to "Never Read Land." Or, if they *do* actually read the book, they will often skip over the parts they feel are unimportant.

But *you*, Noble Reader, are a cut above the pseudo-literary in that you believe that if you do not read *all* the words I have written, then you may not be getting your money's worth. You are to be commended for your insistence on thoroughness and dedication to integrity.

I am trying to imagine what you might be doing while you are reading this book. If you are a pre-bedtime reader, I envision that you are possibly snug beneath your Qualofil comforter (none of those pesky down feathers), reading with a light that is not bright enough (perhaps it's time to upgrade your bulb), and a cup of your favorite tea. Of course, this presents a problem, in that, should you read long enough to make yourself pleasantly sleepy, you will have to decide whether to get up and brush your teeth or risk the tooth decay and tea stain. Eventually, the dental guilt will probably send you to the bathroom, where you will be sufficiently awakened to make you need to read more—but it's just not the same without the tea.

I would hope that some of you are bona fide Beach Readers. You know who you are. My husband is one of your species. He will purchase a book weeks before we go to the beach and save it so that he can read *that* book in *that* spot. He dutifully resists all temptation to read a single word ahead of time, as that would spoil the whole thing. As much as he is committed to deferred gratification, he more firmly believes in the power of the surf to make a magical book even more so. I think this is madness. First of all, no book is a better read when there is sand attached. And you will inevitably get sunscreen on it somewhere. See? Now that you're looking, you see those sunscreen thumbprints on the cover and the edges of the pages, don't you? If the sand sticks to the sunscreen, you have just ruined a perfectly good book. Also, I sunburn easily, so please take me back to the shade.

Some of you are Car Readers. You might be with a group of friends who are headed out for a girlie weekend (this is acceptable only if you are female). There's always one girl who brings along a book and reads funny quips from it *the whole trip*. Hopefully this is not the same person who is The Carsick One. If you are The Carsick One, put the book down. If you are The Driver, put the book down.

So, thanks for lining up with me at the start line. I hope that at the finish line you will think, *I need to give one of these to (insert name of whomever really needs a lift)*. It just inspires me to know that this book will go with you to places I never could physically go, and however much I would like to believe that one of my imaginative scenarios is your reading experience, I am just enough of a realist to know that many of you will be reading this in your "Other Library," "Loo," "Powder Room," or "Water Closet." And that's okay with me, just as long as it doesn't end up underneath the six back issues of *Sports Illustrated* and *Good Housekeeping*, aka "Never Read Land."

so, enough
about me

Remember the one about the conceited person at the luncheon who went on and on about himself? At the end of his recounting of his various wonderful qualities, he said to his lunch date, "Enough about me. Tell me what you think of me."

If you are hyper-pious, you might have already been offended by the book's subtitle. So let me let you know that I know the same thing you know: ultimately, it's not about me; it's all about God. I get that.

But haven't we heard for years that we are all of infinite worth to God because He sent Jesus to die for us? Haven't we been told that if we were the *only one*, He still would have come? It's difficult to fathom that although in the grand scope of eternity I am insignificant, in His eyes I am worth everything.

I love it when people are trying to describe a situation in which they are acutely aware of God's providence in their circumstance and they say, "It was such a God thing." I try to keep a straight face and continue listening, because what I really want to say is, "As if anything isn't."

Sunrises are God things (although I've only seen a couple — "not a morning person" doesn't even begin to describe it), air is a God thing, coffee is a God thing, and my times of intimacy with my husband definitely fall into that category. Watermelons, chocolate, music, hot baths, good music, great friends, autumn evenings, Dippin' Dots ice cream, cloud formations — I believe that they are *all* pretty much "God things" only slightly interrupted by "Satan things."

Most times I can't tell the difference until the experience has long passed and time has sifted through the motives and emotions swirling around the circumstances. Sometimes when I thought something was a blessing from the hand of God, it turned out to be an idol in disguise. Sometimes I thought a circumstance was a plague visited on me from Satan, but it turned out to be a trial that turned to gold. Even the "Satan things" were used to instruct me, discipline me, and help me recognize God's voice. Make no mistake about this one thing: I know that God is real and He is the Holy Center of All. Therefore, all the musings, observations, opinions, and rants in the pages ahead are my own. Unless you are reading an actual Scripture from the actual Bible, pretty much everything else is someone's experience. This book reflects my experiences, twisted as they may be.

Also, I have a life view that entails the deeply held belief that God smiles more than He frowns. I cannot go to the mat theologically for this supposition, but I do know that we are told in Nehemiah 8:10 that "the joy of the LORD is your strength." From this I am guessing that we were meant to be strong and that our joy quotient has a lot to do with our spiritual fitness.

Some church people seem to believe that it is more "spiritual" to be serious and uptight. I realize that there are times when we need to weep and mourn, but the Word of God says that the mourners "will be comforted" (Matthew 5:4) and that "weeping may endure for a night, but joy comes in the morning" (Psalm 30:5, AMP). Sadness and angst were never meant to be our permanent default. And though I know that Jesus was "a man of sorrows, and familiar with suffering" (Isaiah 53:3), I also know that someone who was a grouchy killjoy wouldn't have gotten in trouble for accepting invitations to too many parties and wouldn't have attracted children. I see Him not scowling but smiling when He told His disciples on board their fishing boat after He had calmed the storm, "What a tiny amount of faith you have after all we've been through together" (see Luke 8:25).

I take my faith very seriously. I take God very seriously. The God I've come into relationship with must have lots to laugh about from this girl on a daily basis. He made me like this and He loves me. That makes me full of joy.

in front
of God and
everybody

M ost of my life has been an open book, so it seems only natural to finally write it down. I have a knack for saying the wrong thing at the right time, and it usually makes people laugh (right after they blush).

I remember when I was a child and my aunts would discuss someone's very public foible. They would describe the action as happening "right in front of God and everybody." That is how I feel I live my life—first before the God who made me, knows me, and accepts me, and then in front of everybody else.

Because I am a fully formed female armed with the newfound freedom that only being over forty can bring, I think it's about time that I sit down and pontificate upon some of the wisdom that has accumulated alongside my collection of cellulite. If you are under forty, I want to make it perfectly clear that you will probably feel about this book the way most people feel when they're reading *National Geographic*: it's a wonderful account of someone else's journey to a place you've never been. But just hang on, sistah.

If God lets you live long enough, you'll outgrow that cuteness that has gotten you in and out of many a situation and eagerly trade it in for some secure sassiness that will serve you well as you develop your patina (according to Webster, "a surface appearance of something grown beautiful especially with age or use"). That layer of living makes us truly beautiful and valuable. For those of you who have survived the forty mark and are slapping on your patina faster than pantyhose spring a runner, I know you will know what I'm talking about.

The year that I was forty, I refused to call it forty. I preferred to call it "$39.95 plus shipping and handling." And my, oh my, how my contents had settled during all the shipping and handling. Gravity will have its way. And what a thin-minded century in which to start settling. In every century prior to this one, ample women were considered to be *more* desirable. It was a sign of affluence to have access to all the starches you wanted. You could even be chosen as a Renaissance supermodel based solely on the fact that you had multiple tummy rolls or thunderous thighs. If you had the jiggly tummy, the big thighs, *plus* the derriere to inspire a rap song, you were considered a triple threat and worthy of oil on canvas. Of course, there were no Polaroid cameras back then, so perhaps those women were skinny and the painters just wanted to make them more beautiful so they painted on extra fat. Can you imagine that? A time before Ultra Slim-Fast shakes when *more* was more beautiful? (Mona Lisa may have been too skinny to be painted full body so Leonardo showed her from only the neck up.) But there were also no Pampers back then, no antibiotics, no automobiles, and no Snickers bars. I guess every century has its trade-offs.

After turning forty, I entered into a phase of my life in which Psalm 139:14 had deeper meaning for me. The phrase "*fear*fully and *wonder*fully made" describes exactly how I feel when I look in the mirror. I fear what is happening and I wonder what I can do about it. I'm conflicted as I consider that the very thing keeping my wrinkles fluffed out is the same stuff causing this strange dimpling around my knees. I keep thinking I can blame some of it on the *Prayer of Jabez* book, where we were instructed to ask God to "enlarge our territory." Perhaps I should have been a little more specific.

There are days when I think I might be a "reverse anorexic," meaning that I look in the mirror and see myself much thinner than I actually am. Then I see myself in a picture and realize the truth: the scales are frighteningly accurate. I can distinctly remember when I was in my early thirties and I would get pictures of some family event developed. I would sit in my car outside the drugstore, flip through the pictures, and think to myself, *I am so fat!* What I could not imagine then was that someday I would look back at those *same* pictures and say to myself, *I was looking so fine back in the day!* And I just know down deep in my heart that five years from now I'll be thinking the same thing about those pictures I got developed this week. Life has a way of making last year's fat weight into this year's goal weight.

My family recently took a little tour of Graceland, home of Elvis Presley. The one thing that impressed me about that educational excursion was the fact that *nowhere* in that monument to The King of Rock was a single fat picture of Elvis. I just pray that my children love me that much when I pass on. May they have a photo-burning party and say, "Let's just keep the good ones and honor Mama." If I raised them right, my memory will be preserved without disgrace.

One of the happy advantages to this stage of life is figuring out what sort of stuff you're now too old for. I have given up lots of things like wearing shoes that don't feel good (well, not entirely—I just refuse to wear them for more than an hour), trying on swimsuits, saving wrapping paper, and owning bathroom scales. I also no longer shop at Victoria's Secret because they don't carry any bras in my current size, 38 long.

I'm not saying that we shouldn't help the things we *can* help, but this is a very difficult thing to determine. If it were easy, that very famous prayer wouldn't end with the phrase "and the wisdom to know the difference." We've all seen those makeovers where you can hardly recognize the person from the "before" picture. I dream of someone doing that to me, but I'm so bossy that I probably wouldn't like the end result just because I didn't think it up.

And I worry about the long-term effects of some of the procedures women use these days to fight wrinkles. I'm thinking particularly about the Botox injections. Does it occur to anyone else that we are injecting a chemical classified as a weapon of mass destruction into our faces? And who's to say that it's not leaching out of the dermis into our brains and making us crazy? As if hormones were not enough! Skip the Botox; grow some bangs.

I now have a front-car seat on the hormonal roller coaster called perimenopause. This is a new medical term science has given to the condition that immediately precedes full-blown, hot-flashin', mood-swingin', drug-takin' menopause. In this new "lite" version, you get all the same symptoms, just without the regularity. In other words, you never know when it's going to hit you. Menopause is basically your hormonally messed-up teenage years revisited and complicated by the fact that you are perpetually tired and have a mortgage.

I am just beginning to figure out that women in full-blown menopause must have to time their hot flashes to avoid putting on their makeup at the wrong time. If you have a hot flash while applying your makeup, it will melt on contact. And you may not be aware of this, but if you have a hot flash while wearing knee-high boots, you can actually cook your calves. Don't laugh—it can happen. Scientists could resolve the whole global-warming debate by admitting that the cause is the number of female Baby Boomers reaching this "power surge" stage of life. And if a calorie is a measurement of heat converted to usable energy, why don't hot flashes burn extra calories? We could just hot-flash our way down to size four and still ingest unlimited supplies of Krispy Kremes to offset those manic mood swings. That would seem more fair, don't you think?

Surprisingly, I've read about women who want to have babies around the age of fifty. I do not understand this. I can't fathom what sort of rationale would entertain the possibility of a labor pain happening concurrent with a hot flash.

I have read many magazine articles that state that one way to avoid the effects of menopause is to "accessorize." Or maybe it was "exercise." Whatever. I've always had a personal aversion to any activity that leads to perspiration. This is one of those issues that divides the population into two distinct camps. There are people, like my friend Jennifer, who believe that to sweat is one of the most fulfilling things you can do. She actually uses up valuable brain cells thinking up ways to do even *more* of these things that lead to sweating and then schedules them into her Daytimer. Don't get me wrong. I admire her. She has even encouraged me to attend her cardio kickboxing class, which was a disaster. It's not even my fault, because I'm a product of my genetics. When nondancing Baptists intermarry with even more nondancing Baptists, eventually all the rhythmic genes are totally bred out of your lineage, and "massive failure to dance" is the result. I am borderline spastic (my children would disagree with the "borderline" part), and exercise is just not graceful for me. I have to actually concentrate to keep from falling off the treadmill. And my philosophy about exercise does not line up with conventional wisdom. The experts say, "No pain, no gain." I say, "No pain, no p-a-i-n." The fitness magazines say, "Warm up, kick it up, work it out, cool down." I say, "Start slow and then taper off." I do have some great-looking athletic shoes, though. They give the impression that at any moment I just might break out into a marathon-worthy run if I had a mind to.

Do you remember how way back in the 1980s the big deal was aerobics? We put on our Jazzercise tights and bounced around to "Boogie Woogie Bugle Boy" and thought we were doing ourselves all sorts of favors. Then we all got older and realized there had to be a better way of getting fit than jumping up and down, increasing our sagging quotient.

Now the rage is Pilates. That's my kind of exercise. The first thing you have to do in Pilates class is lie down.

So let me just sum it up and save us all years of emotional energy, because this is the truth: today you are wonderful. This level of acceptance will set you free to stop worrying about the inevitable effects of gravity. And a helpful hint: if you tilt your head and stick out your chin a little, you'll look better in all your pictures.

purse-onality

Traditional wisdom states, "You are what you eat," and, "Clothes make the (wo)man." But any chick worth her Premarin knows that the truer truism is "You are your purse." We know this because we have felt overwhelming panic at the thought that we may have lost our purse. This feeling is normally reserved for the possibility that we may have misplaced a passport or a child. In death, you can't take it with you *when* you go, but in life you *can* take it with you *as* you go.

Our purses are a combination of form, function, and fashion. Sometimes it takes years of searching for just the right one that is roomy enough for our necessities without being too big, has just the right number of compartments, transmits just the right message about our classiness/funkiness, and looks good on us when we carry it. This is a distinctly female phenomenon. We "try on" purses. This is why there are mirrors in the handbag department. A purse *must* look good on us. Notice that there are no mirrors in the guy's wallet or backpack department.

Although drawstring pouches have been a part of history back to the ancients, our modern idea of a handbag is as recent as the Second World War, when women entered the workplace and needed to have their things with them during the workday. Nevertheless, I believe that in the early chapters of Genesis—where it says that after sin entered the world, God killed an animal and made leather clothes for Eve—surely there must have been a purse to complete her ensemble.

Some women insist on calling their purse a "pocketbook." This seems bizarre to me, as it is neither a "pocket" nor a "book." Discuss amongst yourselves.

Purses are sacrosanct. Girls dare not go through the purse of even their best friend. Who knows what secrets lie inside? Magicians don't reveal their methods; girls don't spill their purses. In the movie *How to Lose a Guy in Ten Days*, the guys had to "accidentally" knock the female character's purse over to get to the contents, as none of them had the courage to reach a hand inside. Purses are mysterious to men of all ages. Though John and I have been married a long time, he will still bring my purse to me so that I can retrieve something rather than look in there himself. Smart man.

My first encounter with the netherworld of purse and contents was with my grandmother's purse, which was shiny brown vinyl with a snap closure and cloth lining. My mom sang in the choir at church, so I would sit with my grandmother in the pew and try to keep still (so as not to risk her pinching wrath). As riveting as the pastor's message may have been (cough, cough), nothing interested me as much as the inside of Nana's purse. The contents didn't change much from week to week; I just liked opening it and peering into the darkness. She usually carried a couple of clean tissues, some loose wintergreen Lifesavers, a couple of folded one dollar bills (she never carried a wallet then as she didn't get her driver's license until my granddad passed away), loose pennies and nickels, a pencil from the hardware store, and a pen from the bank. And there were always individual sticks of Juicy Fruit gum. The aroma from the wintergreen seemed to taint the flavor of the Juicy Fruit due to their cohabitation in an unwrapped state, but I chewed the gum anyway.

I don't think I was actually "purse conscious" until I was about six years old, and then only to tote my offering to church and start my own Juicy Fruit stash. When you are in grade school, a purse isn't really a necessity. This is because in grade school, life is not terribly complicated. No bills, no stamps, no lipstick, no ID, no worries. Once you reach the age of feminine hygiene, however, your purse is a matter of life or death. We spend our lives looking for the perfect camouflage pouch for our stuff so that we can avoid the humiliation and degradation should the contents be inadvertently toppled out for public viewing.

And girls start early with purse psychology. We judge our acquaintances by their purse-onality. You know you've done it. You've sized up a woman based on what was slung on her shoulder, clutched in her hand, or dangling from her forearm. And in truth, you can tell a lot about a woman based on what she comes toting.

Some are the "I-need-everything-with-me-at-all-times" chicks.

These are the girls who take the "always prepared" credo just a smidge too far. Depending on their age, life station, diet status, and number of children, they could be carrying around a veritable pharmacy, cosmetics counter, 7-Eleven snack aisle, and various articles of clothing.

I was at a ladies' event a few months ago and they were playing a sort of "Let's Make a Deal" game, asking for women to find certain items in their purse. Some of the requests were outrageous, some pretty tame. One of the tamer requests was for women to come up to the stage if they had some article (other than a picture) in their purse that showed their child's sports team. Three women bolted toward the stage. One had a coupon book that the team was selling, another had a key fob with the team logo on it, and a third had her son's athletic supporter (it was clean). Does this take the term "soccer mom" to a whole new dimension?

There are also the Tiny Toters. They would never compromise their delicate sensibilities with a large bag. They consider it a social faux pas to leave their vehicle with anything larger than an itty-bitty wisp of a bag. These are almost always the Trim Women, and they want a little bag that corresponds to their body size. They carry only a single, perfect lipstick, a thin wallet, and a slimline mirror. If there is a key in that bag, it is the one that opens the door of the car, and they leave all their other keys inside the glove compartment. They might also have a single tissue in there. It would be folded in order to maximize space.

These are the same women who got by with the extra-small

diaper bags. I remember looking in wonder at the Tiny Toter moms at the morning-out program at our church. They brought in their diaper bags that were no bigger than a book. They would have two slim diapers in there, a flat pack of wipes, individually wrapped crackers, and (of course) a Capri Sun. My kids had the rolling footlocker when I dropped them off—it contained eighteen pacifiers, a six-pack of apple juice, an entire package of Huggies, and their favorite toys (in case that particular nursery room was woefully inadequate). In a Tiny Toter, you've got yourself a bona fide minimalist with a mile-wide control streak. But if these women ever need a place to hide anything, they are tough outa luck.

I've also long been intrigued by women who go strapless. These handheld purses require a lot of mental energy. If it's not parked on your shoulder, you really have to be mindful not to lay it down somewhere and forget it—just like babies.

Some girls are what I like to call "serial monogamists." These are the ones who will buy one purse and stick with it until it wears out. Only then will they give themselves permission to buy another one. They're also the type who never move their furniture just for fun. These women are the sort that make great friends, as they are loyal unto death.

Then we have the purse schizophrenics (they have a Purse-onality Disorder). These ladies have a purse to fit any mood, and they often change their purses out during a single twenty-four-hour period. You can never count on the contents of their purse from day to day as they will admit, "Oh, I left it in my other purse." You might not want to trust them with your airline tickets, but you definitely would want them with you on vacation. These are the fun chicks.

I have seen pictures of my ritzy aunt from Dallas that were taken during the late 1960s, and she always had a purse and shoes that matched. Same fabric. (Does that mean they were "sole mates"?) That would never do these days. We could not pull off such amazing matchy-matchiness.

Purse taste can be regionally influenced. I was shocked when I was in the Midwest and discovered that women there carry fabric purses that have no correlation to their wardrobe. In fact, they have no shame that the print on their Vera Bradley (quilted, expensive) bags clashes with whatever print they may be wearing. That is why Vera Bradley bags will never really catch on in the South as your everyday purse. We like it when our purse matches our outfit, but at the very least it shouldn't clash.

I've been through lots of purse phases in my life. I had a solitary leather purse throughout my high school years and then several purse/backpack combinations throughout college. My diaper bag *was* my purse for about seven years of my kids' babyhoods. I then entered a strange phase where I had this cockeyed notion that a basket would make a great purse. During this time, I perpetually resembled Little Red Riding Hood. I was able to tote a lot, but no one can really respect a chick with her stuff in a basket. To over-correct this phase, I shifted into the "Dayrunner Only" mode. (I think I was hoping that something would happen in my life that was worthy of writing down in my planner.) For the last several years, I have been in the "something a little short of a suitcase" mode. I love bucket bags that you can just dump all your stuff into.

Purse contents are sneaky. It doesn't seem possible that inanimate objects would have intelligence, but I believe they can feel you reaching in and they take evasive action by sliding over to the opposite side. They do this until you get really irritated and dump the entire contents of your purse out on the bed. As frustrated as you are, you are secretly glad you are forced to clean out your purse.

I daily dump and regroup. My husband is mystified by this behavior. He also doesn't understand how my car can get so messy. I tried to explain that women just think of our automobiles as a mobile extension of our purse—a "Purse on Wheels," so to speak. There was a long shaking of the head.

So as you peruse the plethora of purse diversity, refuse to purchase any purse that does not resonate with your Purse-onality. If there's a lid for every pot, then there's a purse for every chick. Follow your Purse Bliss.

you're as young as you're ever gonna be

I can't believe the stuff I drop money on in the cosmetics department of Walgreens. It's that no-questions-asked return policy
they have that lures me in. It makes me feel I can be a fearless
shopper when it comes to makeup and toiletries. Did the shade of
lipstick you chose resemble the safety cones on the roadside when
you got it home? No problem. Walgreens will take it back. Did
the bubble bath promise to send you into bath-time nirvana but
leave you with a rash instead? No problem. Walgreens will take
it back. I've had some great fearless purchases, and I've had some
real doozies.

I actually bought something called "Weight Reducing Cream"
in a lovely pearlescent tube. Right there on the tube is printed,
"Lose Pounds and Inches" and "Controls Appetite, Increases
Metabolism, Firms and Flattens." Honey, if there was somethin' in a tube that could do all that, wouldn't *you* trot it right
up to the counter and lay down your hard-earned dollars? I had
visions of myself actually losing weight while sleeping or—even

better!—losing weight *while* eating dinner. If we live in the era of land rovers on Mars, could simultaneous eating and losing weight be too farfetched?

Well, I got the stuff home, popped the top, and just knew I was gonna be firmed and flattened by daybreak! Wasn't Oprah just gonna call me right up and ask me to be on her "Amazing Transformations" segment in a week or two? Maybe I should dig out the digital camera and take some "before" pictures just in case.

According to the directions, I was supposed to rub a quarter-size dollop onto my tummy and "other problem areas" one hour prior to eating. (Don't they know that at a certain age, they're *all* "problem areas"?) So I slathered a good palmful onto my "areas" (everything between my boobs and my knees), reasoning that if a quarter-size dollop were good, wouldn't *seven* quarters be better? I felt sure that I would shrink before I got to REM.

Problem is, I never actually got to sleep that night. I felt exactly like I had overdosed on Sudafed as I flopped like a chicken on the rotisserie all night long. I was trying to sleep but felt like a live wire still hooked up to the power plant. After three exhausting hours of this, I got up in the middle of the night with heart palpitations, certain I was having some sort of cardiac incident, and tried to read the ingredients. Only then did I notice the fine print: the actively absorbed agent was none other than caffeine. I had smeared the equivalent of fifteen cups of coffee on my "problem areas." In this product's defense, I did lose weight from the bed gymnastics.

I believe that there's not much a girl won't do if the promise includes holding back the hands of time or erasing the marks that time has already made on her. I know I'm susceptible to the miraculous cream claims and the appeal of youth. But isn't the definition of "young" getting a good bit more youthful every year? Supermodels are told that their careers are over at the ripe old age of twenty-five.

It is hard to help my teenage daughter navigate this profoundly shallow culture. When every other television show is built around the premise of surgical enhancements and "extreme makeovers," it's a chore to convince a girl of any age that beauty is something deeper than a plastic surgeon can touch and that she radiates true beauty every time she shows love and compassion. (I wonder why we never see a TV show about that.) But I have come to a place of some acceptance in my life via the thought that no matter how old I feel, I'm as young as I'm ever gonna be. Think about that carefully: you will never be any younger than you are at this moment. Hello!

Age is relative anyway. For instance, if you are eighteen and it is your destiny to be taken from this life at the age of twenty-one, you may *think* you're young, but in reality most of your life has already been lived. That makes you old. On the other hand, if you are fifty-eight and you are going to live to be a hundred, you're young (proportionately). The point is, none of us knows how long we might live or how old that really makes us, so why not celebrate how young you might be? As Satchel Paige said, "How old would you be if you didn't know how old you are?"

I have known some aged people who are very young inside.

Marge Caldwell from Houston is a vibrant sprite of a woman who sparkles and giggles when she talks and is going on ninety years young. She is a woman who knows that age is just a number on a driver's license. Conversely, I have known some teenagers and college students who by virtue of the weight of life upon them seemed as if they were very, very old.

This notion of today being my youngest day of the rest of my life makes me want to try to turn cartwheels, live a little more daringly, celebrate everything with a bit more gusto, and fully appreciate the gift of life. So today I will skip the caffeine body cream and maybe call a friend as I pour a second cup of fresh-brewed java.

Youth is not in a number, or in a night cream, or in a surgeon's scalpel. It's in your head and your heart. Be as mature as you must, but refuse to be any older than you are. Don't let this youngest day of the rest of your life go by without a little celebration!

funny-bone
archaeology

A lot of people ask questions about being funny. They want to know if I was "always funny," or when I knew that I was funny, or if I was the class clown in school. I, my very own self, sometimes wonder how I got to be doing this thing of helping people reclaim their long-lost belly laugh, so I might be writing this chapter so I can figure out the mystery.

I was born under not-so-funny circumstances. My mom, in order to escape an alcoholic father, married my birth father just out of high school. He was unfaithful to her throughout their brief marriage and left when I was too young to remember it. So when I arrived, though I'm sure my mother was happy to see me, it was not under the best of emotional conditions. When I was two, my mom and I moved in with Nana (pronounced "na-naw") and Granddad. My mom was devastated by the turn of events that had left her a single mom and felt that it might just be next to impossible to trust a man ever again. She went to work in her older brother's building supply company, handling accounts payable and trying to feel whole again. So it would be for the next six years.

I grew up on a farm with some cows, various dogs and cats, a vegetable garden, flower beds, and a big oak tree in the front yard that had a hole in it that acted like a rainwater barrel. That hole was very mysterious to me. We also had well water, as we were a good five miles outside of town, and would occasionally have a frog fall into the well and decompose. The smell of the decomposing frog was awful. We couldn't use the well water for several days until it cleared up. Such was life in the country.

I have a very clear recollection of standing on a tree stump down close to an area we called "The Pecan Bottom," where there was a stand of pecan trees. It was about a football field's length from the farmhouse, but you could still see the house. It was as far as I was allowed to go. I would stand out there on that tree stump and sing loudly to whatever cows happened to be chewing their cud nearby. I remember thinking that they didn't seem too impressed, but I didn't care. The song was in my heart, and a girl had to let it fly somewhere.

By this time, my granddad had decided that he needed to give his messed-up life to Christ, so he was no longer a raging alcoholic. He was more of a broken-down man with a terrible temper and myriad health problems as a result of his years of alcohol abuse. Before his body was a mess, he had been a canta- loupe and watermelon farmer. He and my nana had raised nine children during the Great Depression, and part of the family's survival was due to the fact that my taskmaster granddad worked all his kids in the fields. He was a natural-born salesman when it came to his watermelons and cantaloupes, and he tried to manage a short-lived family trio (comprised of my mom, her twin, and the baby sister accompanied by the youngest boy on the piano). Their talent and harmonies were wonderful, but by the time he needed them to have stage-worthy self-confidence, his rages had taken most of it out of them.

But I was the apple of his eye. I got to be the recipient of the love and encouragement he could never allow himself to give his own children. By the time I was four, I was singing in church with my mother. They would stand me on a folding chair so we could share the microphone, and my granddad would be beaming from the congregation. Afterward, he would slip me a dollar and drive me to the gas station to buy an ICEE, the absolute best treat in the central Texas heat. Thus, I began a career in music. Sometimes I still get paid in food.

Of course, I firmly believe that my mother wouldn't have even made it to adolescence, much less adulthood, had it not been for the strength of Nana. My mother was severely asthmatic as a child and had pneumonia several times. They had no money for doctors, so my mother struggled through illness for much of her childhood. She missed weeks of school because of it and still hates spelling. Nana did the best she could to doctor her brood and keep bodies and souls together. This woman (who married at fifteen and was pregnant for twenty years) was the bedrock of our family. And she had seen enough hard times before the age of twenty to kill a lesser person. But Nana found her strength in God and did whatever was necessary, not only to survive, but to bless others. If you were to ask my mom's brothers and sisters, each would have his or her own story of a time when Nana would somehow manage to come up with whatever was needed. Her resourcefulness was nothing short of miraculous. She would sell eggs and save enough to help her sons buy engagement rings.

Nana also had a reputation as a fine cook. She could make the fluffiest rolls and the best roast you ever wrapped your lips around. She loved to feed people in general, but she got her greatest joy from feeding preachers. I think she felt she owed her very existence to the fact that someone told her about a hope that went beyond this life and that one of the ways she could show her gratitude was to feed the people who delivered that message on a regular basis. My nana always had a heart for preachers. Good thing, too, because three of her sons grew up to be them. My mom recalls many days when half the church (a small church) would come home with them for Sunday dinner. Nana could lay an abundant spread and multiply the loaves and fishes (or fluffy rolls and roast, as the case was).

Church was the centerpiece of our lives, and though our church was long on doctrine, it was decidedly short on joy. I don't know if it was the result of a dogma borne of hard times, but laughter was not appreciated and hardly tolerated, much less encouraged. It might have been okay for the preacher to say something amusing during a sermon, but it was never called a "joke," and if anyone *else* said something funny, it was most likely a sin. I believe that the reasoning went something like this: if you laugh, you must be experiencing pleasure, and if you're experiencing pleasure, it must be a sin; therefore, laughter equals sin. Oh, they never actually said this, but it was one of those unspoken rules that everyone knew and no one questioned. Our faith culture was very rigid and well defined by rules that were all about length: length of hair (men, short; women, long); length of your skirt (women, long; men, don't go there); length of your daily Bible reading time (everyone, as long as you can); length of time in church or spent at the altar praying (same as above). There was safety in knowing the rules. It was easier to gauge your obedience to God if you knew the requirements and you didn't really have to think too much. And so it was that I was brought up with many, many rules and not much sense that God made *anyone* funny (and if He did, we must beat it out of them).

This all radically changed the day that John Pulliam entered our lives. My mom had been raising me without any financial (or other) support from my birth father for six years. During this time (even in the cheerless church), I had come to understand that I needed Jesus in my life in order to escape hell. It's not the *best* reason to ask Him to forgive you and begin your own relationship with the God of the Universe, but I see it like getting married. Some people don't get married under the best of circumstances, but if you are committed to the relationship, you can grow to love someone in the way he or she deserves to be loved. God deserved a love from me that was more than fire insurance, but I would grow into it only later.

I remember the night I made that decision to receive Christ as my Savior. I was eight years old and in a service that my uncle was preaching. I knew that I had sinned (I had lied to my mom, taken money from her purse, various childhood felonies of that sort), and I knew that there was no way to absolve that guilt inside myself. I was also made aware, through various stories of young people being killed in tragic car accidents (that was an evangelist's stock in trade — stories of teenage automobile crashes), that I could die in this unforgiven state. So I headed down to the altar to deal with it. I remember asking Jesus to forgive me and feeling like I had just done the most joyous thing in my life to that point (including getting a bike with a banana seat and plastic streamers on the handlebars the previous Christmas). When we were on our way home, I sat on the armrest of my mom's Caprice between her and my uncle. I felt like a freshly minted, shiny copper penny, all clean inside and out.

During the years that my mom was single, my nana prayed that God would send her the gift of a husband — one who would love her, be trustworthy, and be a good father to me. A new guy moved into our tiny town of Burnet, Texas, about fifty miles northwest of Austin in the Hill Country. Every year, the bluebonnets and Indian paintbrush put on a spectacle of color (God showing off), but otherwise, it is hilly, rocky, and mostly the color of dirt, with a couple of beautiful lakes thrown in for relief. The town was home to less than two thousand people, so it was possible to know just about everyone in Burnet.

Mom met the new guy in the choir at First Baptist Church. After their first date (to a Burnet Bulldogs high school football game), they both knew that God had brought them together. They were married a few months later, and my mom literally giggled her way down the aisle. I think that was the first time I had ever seen that. My mom was happy, and I felt sure that I would be, too.

So it was that John Pulliam became my stepfather and I got acquainted with a different breed of relatives. I was inducted into a new sort of family that loved laughter and would egg each other on to a fever pitch. My new grandmother, Ludie Monk Pulliam, was one of several sisters who could literally laugh till they wet their underpants (and loved it!). My stepdad and his sister, Louise, would laugh their way past audible sound into the silent wheezing zones, where they would have to wipe away the tears from laughing so hard. These fits of frivolity were a delectable taste of freedom for my mom and me. We were now part of a family that loved laughter.

It wasn't until I graduated from college that I had my first experiences in "professional" humor. I got a job at a Christian radio station in Jackson, Mississippi, and shared the morning drive-time program with one of the station owners. We did a lot of pretty silly stuff in attempts to increase the listenership. That was my first taste of "goofy on purpose," and I was hooked. Within a couple of years, I was beginning to lead worship at a few area women's events and inevitably something would strike me funny during the course of the singing and I would just say out loud what most of the people were already thinking. The ladies seemed to enjoy some relief from the heavy topics that were the usual fare at those sorts of conferences, and word got around that they should get Anita to "come and do some of that funny stuff." After a while, they asked me to come and do *all* funny stuff. I'm not sure if they were truly trying to encourage my gift or if they just didn't have the guts to tell me that I couldn't sing all that well. Whichever it was, God opened up opportunities for me to develop in an area that I never imagined He would choose to use. I have the great pleasure of traveling to countless places, meeting so many people, and sharing hope through humor. I still get up in the morning unable to believe that God allows me to bring the gift of laughter to so many who are looking for real joy.

I have heard it said that laughter is the shortest distance between two hearts. If that is true, then you don't have to unearth funny bones in your family's archives in order to span the distance. Anyone can laugh, so go ahead and let your funny bone stick out. We all have access to the shortcut between hearts. What a trip!

embracing your inner weirdness

I remember when I was a teenager and felt that singularly defining angst of adolescence: that feeling that you will never quite fit in and that life must be great for those people who look as if they are fitting in really well.

There are a couple of things I wish I had known back then:

1. Everybody else felt the same way.
2. This feeling magically dissipates when you come to embrace the wonderful weirdness that makes you "you."

Our society in general doesn't celebrate uniqueness, unless you are rich. In that case, people you would deem weird if they were your next-door neighbors are upgraded to the classification of "eccentric" due to their wealth. This is one of the labels that money *can* buy.

From the time we are rolled into the nursery, footprinted,

blood-typed, and given a birth certificate, we are systematically fed through the tubes of conformity until we lose our distinctives and become another cookie-cutter-two-dimensional-second-cousin-twice-removed version of ourselves. We are told not to laugh too loudly, call attention to ourselves, or make a scene. "Can't you just fit in?" Of course, my husband grew up in Mississippi, where the truly eccentric become famous novelists. I envy that sometimes.

If you understand who you are and who God made you to be, then it doesn't mess with you when others are who God made them to be. My mom, my daughter, and I share some similarities. We all love ice cream, laugh at chick flicks, love to read books, and believe that any time spent in pajamas is quality time. However, we are totally distinct. My mom L-O-V-E-S to do laundry. I let her! I dress sorta funky; my daughter is more Ann Taylor-ish. My daughter loves hockey; I don't understand it at all. We are all exactly as God intended, and isn't it splendid?

Our churches don't really know what to do with those who are not afraid of individuality, either. It's easier to tow the "Stepford believer" line than to make room for those whose thought processes and forms of expression don't quite fit the unspoken "norm." This standard varies from church to church, and if you fall outside that mode of decorum, you are dangerous and to be avoided at best or labeled a "heretic" at worst. Oh, not officially. Just behind the eyes.

If people's expectations of us put us "in a box," then it seems to me that we spend a good deal of our time on earth just swapping boxes. We get some knowledge in one area of our life and realize that we have been enslaved to an idea or expectation. We leave that mindset, only to find that we miss the structure the box afforded us, so we find another one to climb into. We say that we don't like them, but we keep climbing in.

Boxes seem safer than dance floors, don't they?

Rules are easier to understand than grace.

Grace is dangerous. It is about unleashing, not about controlling.

What's strange about this mindset is that it is juxtaposed against a Bible in which many of those celebrated as giants in the faith were somewhat . . . er . . . shall we say . . . "different"?

John the Baptist — now this was a cat with major fashion and dietary issues. He was a standout, and his message was plain. He cut a wide swath proclaiming that Jesus was on the way. Was he weird? You bet. Was he true to his mission? Absolutely. Would you have invited him to your block party? Probably not.

Peter was a roughneck fisherman who often put his mouth in gear a good while prior to engaging his brain. He was always making pronouncements about what he was and wasn't going to do. Did any of this keep him from being the front man for the birth of the church? Quite the opposite. It was his roughneck history that made him accessible to the common man. It was his audacity that made him perfect for his calling in his time.

Jesus, above all, knew who He was and exactly what it was that He came here to do. He was labeled a heretic, criticized for ignoring the rules, and crucified for refusing to renounce His identity.

I live in a neighborhood that I sometimes refer to as "communist" partly due to the fact that they regulate everything that occurs outside of our homes. When we moved into Little Moscow, we signed a neighborhood covenant (although there was no slaying of animals to seal the deal), which stated that we would abide by The Code. It covers every possible sort of exterior detail. There are regulation shutter and door colors and regulation mailboxes. There's no removal of trees without approval, no structural changes to the home without approval, no storage sheds, no parking of cars outside of garages, no yard art. Nothin'. We even have a designated weekend approved for our community garage sale. If you happen to be out of town that weekend, then you are just stuck with your junk/treasures for another year. I believe that in the really tiny print, there may have been some references to which sorts of beetles and fireflies were approved for our neighborhood. And the homeowners association will issue a citation if you are in violation of any of the community standards. They have committees that will send you strongly worded letters to deal with any infraction of The Code.

We know this because we got a letter a couple of years ago regarding the fact that there were rocks in our drainage pipe that was at the bottom of our fenced yard. My husband protested that we didn't even *have* a drainage pipe back there. He even called The Code Committee to tell them we didn't have a pipe. They insisted that we did. John marched down there to prove them wrong. Guess what? We *do* have a pipe back there. We had lived here four years and didn't know it. It was covered up with pine straw and rocks. What gets me is that The Code Committee knew. How did they know? This tends to make me believe in a multitude of conspiracy theories. Just what *else* do they know about us?

Imagine if Noah had lived in our subdivision. The citations for a backyard yacht project would have piled up in his regulation mailbox. Talk about unauthorized yard art. Noah's obedience to build a boat in a time when rain and flooding were foreign concepts to the earth made him a little more than slightly irregular. And the fact that he was willing to stay with the plan for years qualifies him as long-term weird. Yet he was God's instrument in preventing the complete eradication of the earth.

Some years back, I had the privilege of meeting Heather Whitestone. (You may remember that she was the first Miss America who was deaf.) This was before her cochlear implant surgery — I think she can hear a little now, but not then. At this conference we were at, she was as beautiful as she had been years earlier during her reign. Her skin looked flawless, her hair perfect and shiny. She wore a silk suit and looked as pretty as a picture.

Heather, an excellent lip-reader, sat down next to me and immediately began a conversation. She asked if I had any children. I answered that I did, and she asked if I had a picture of them. So I pulled out my been-in-my-purse-far-too-long plastic picture holder and showed her my couple of snapshots of my children. She was genuinely kind and interested. I then did what any Southern woman worth her salt would have done: I asked her if she had a picture of her boys. Heather smiled and reached under her chair to retrieve a beautiful oak box.

When she opened the box, I saw two things inside: her Miss America crown and a copy of *People* magazine. I was lost in my wondering about how it must be to carry your crown around with you everywhere you go. I thought that it surely must come in handy when you aren't getting the kind of service you were expecting at the grocery store or if you needed the traffic to move out of your way. You could just whip out your tiara and watch the people scurry in the presence of Bona Fide American Beauty Royalty.

Just then, Heather opened the issue of *People* ("Miss Americas: Where are they now?") to a page with a picture of her holding one of her little boys. She was wearing a beautiful dress, holding her beautiful child, in a magazine known for featuring the beautiful people. If only she could have seen the thought forming in my mind, the bubble would have read, "Our lives couldn't be any more different, could they?"

She replaced the magazine in the oak box, closed the lid, took a couple more bites of her chicken salad, and then touched my arm and asked me, "Can I ask you a question?" Then she pointed to the tiniest red speck on her chin and asked me, "Can you see this pimple?" It was the most miniscule pinprick of a thing, but I remembered how every zit I'd ever had felt so huge (regardless of its actual size), and I answered her, "Not without a microscope."

At that moment, the only thought circling through my head was, *We really are all the same, aren't we?*

Whether we're a former Miss America, a middle-aged homemaker, or a thirteen-year-old girl, we all want to know if something strange is sticking out.

When I was growing up and obsessing about the size of my nose (substantial), my grandmother used to tell me, "It gives you character." I distinctly recall thinking that I could've done with a little less "character." She would also remind me in my insecure moments that people were not thinking about me as much as I imagined they were. She said that they were all doing the same thing I was doing: wondering what others were thinking of *them*. If I could reclaim a chunk of lost time and wasted emotional energy, I would wish to have back all the moments I spent lost in those useless thoughts.

If beauty is in the eye of the beholder, your wonderful uniqueness is precisely what brings God pleasure. It gives you "character" and He's smitten with you. So don't just embrace your uniqueness; revel in it.

you've got
male

I recently read about a study by author Michael Gurian on the ways the brains of men and women are wired differently. The findings, in his book *What Could He Be Thinking? How a Man's Mind Really Works*, are based on years of neurobiological research as well as behavioral observations.

Gurian's contention is that the male brain secretes much less of the powerful primary bonding chemical oxytocin and less of the calming chemical serotonin. Instead, guys get a brainwash of testosterone and vasopressin—pretty much opposite of what the women get. This study said that when it comes to relaxation for a female, the best possible outcome of the day is to wind it down with a deep conversation with your man. The study also concluded that for a man, the worst possible outcome at the end of the day consists of the female's idea of the best possible outcome.

How can this be? Gurian says that his research supports the theory that a man's best relationship is one of "intimate separateness." So we finally have the scientific proof of what we have suspected all along: men want to be intimately committed to someone who will basically just leave them alone.

We've all got male. He may be a husband, son, boss, boyfriend, or coworker, but we all must attempt to relate to him even if we never quite understand him. Some of my girlfriends are single and have hopes of finding a male to love and cherish forever. I hear them talk about the possibilities, and they say things like, "Oh, I'm not sure that I'm ready to meet him. I'm not down to my 'dating weight.'" When I hear them say that, I silently offer up a prayer of thanksgiving that I am ecstatically married.

I've got a really good man, and I mean that sincerely. John brings me coffee every morning. (It's the only way he knows of to get me out of bed.) Isn't coffee just a wonderful invention? God must approve of men making the coffee for the chicks, because He named a whole book in the New Testament "He-Brews." When I smell the coffee being waved under my nose, I know it's time to open my eyes and behold my handsome man. He is fine-looking and still totally turns my crank. For those of you who married a guy who was handsome back in the day and hasn't held up so well, you probably would have benefited from the technology that the FBI uses when they are attempting to find missing children. They scan the youngster's photo in and technologically "age" the subject. That would have come in handy when you were trying to decide if this is the man with whom you wanted to spend the rest of your life.

God knew I needed someone good-looking, loving, patient, and kind. If my male didn't have all of those characteristics (plus a great sense of humor), he definitely would have killed me by now. I will never forget the moment I knew that John was the one for me.

It was 1981, and we were young and in love. It was October, and in Jackson, Mississippi, that means that the state fair comes to town. John and I had been dating about four months and knew that we were in love, but we had yet to determine exactly how much. I do, however, recall wanting him to kiss me almost every time I drew a breath. (If only I could muster that much emotional energy these days. Youth is, indeed, wasted on the young.)

Anyway, we went to the fair after our classes were over at Mississippi College. Oh, the smell of cotton candy, grilled onions and sausages, and caramel apples! And the *piece de resistance*: the Martha White flour biscuits and cane molasses offered for free! Sponsored by Jim Buck Ross and the Mississippi Department of Agriculture, that booth always had a half-mile-long line of people waiting to get those sweet biscuits. The biscuits are warm and tender, the molasses created that very day by mules walking around in circles, grinding up the fresh sugar cane. They pour the cane juice onto large cooking surfaces, where it's reduced to the thick, sweet, sticky bite of heaven itself.

In retrospect, I have often wondered how our young stomachs could handle all that we threw at them while wandering up and down the midway. Full of gyros and funnel cakes and having just come from the Ferris wheel (with a lovely view of downtown Jackson), we were feeling happy that we still had a few dollars in our pockets. Then the hawker invited us under his tent.

His pitch: "Give me ten dollars for the chance at winning this wonderful tool set. How can you lose?" So I asked John for a ten-dollar bill and handed it to the Hawker Man. John stayed back near the edge of the tent. Within seconds, the Hawker Man gave the tool set away to another dollar contributor. Then he said, "For those of you who are left, only twenty dollars more can buy you a chance at this fab-u-lous stereo!"

Who wouldn't want to take advantage of this wonderful opportunity? Of course, I looked back at John and he handed me a twenty with a bemused expression on his face. I knew that this was a sacrifice. We were both college students, and sometimes twenty dollars was the difference between having gas and food or being immobile and hungry. As you could already guess, the stereo went to someone else. But the hawker wasn't done yet. "For only twenty dollars more, each of you can have the chance at winning this be-au-ti-ful color television set." I was in all the way now. Not that I *needed* a TV. I lived at home with my parents, and John already had one in his apartment. But I was so caught up in the moment, I just knew that it would somehow complete my life *and* validate that I hadn't just thrown away all the other money. I couldn't stop now. I was this close.

Besides, the odds were in my favor. Of the twenty or so people standing around handing money to this man, three had already won. And the man kept saying, "Everyone will be a winner. Everyone will win something." Those words reverberated in my head. I knew it was my time to win. I looked back at John with pleading eyes. That was his only money for the rest of the week.

He knew it; I knew it. But wasn't everyone going to be a winner? He handed me his last twenty dollars and, with a slight shake of the head, drifted back to his spot toward the edge of the tent.

I eagerly handed his twenty dollars to the persuasive carnival man. I must have looked like the most eager beaver in the crowd while I waited the twenty seconds it took for him to take twenty-dollar bills from the others left standing. At this point, almost everyone had cut their losses and departed from the front area to console themselves with a Pronto Pup corn dog. I was thrilled! I now had *much* better odds at winning. There were only a few of us remaining at the front. I was a shoo-in! I waited with bated breath as the man pulled the ticket stub from the bowl and called out a different number than mine. My heart sank. But wasn't everyone going to win *something*? The man started passing out the consolation prizes. He handed me a curio cabinet about thirty inches high and ten inches across made out of pressboard and plastic. All told, it was worth about $4.50, if that.

I looked at it, incredulous that I had just blown fifty bucks on something so lame. I was afraid to turn around and face John. I just knew he was going to have some sort of weird mix of consternation over my blowing his last dime, disappointment in my lack of ability to discern a swindle when I saw one, and general loss of faith in his new love. I teared up just thinking about the lecture formulating in his head and well deserved on my part. With a heavy heart, I turned around to face the music.

There is no rational explanation for what happened next, except that some people have a great capacity for grace. When I sheepishly searched for John's face near the back of the tent, all I could see was his neck because he had his head fully thrown back, laughing out loud. He wasn't mad. He wasn't disappointed in me. He hadn't lost faith in me. He was laughing. I knew I had found the love of my life.

That curio cabinet still hangs in our house. It is a testament to love and grace. I am one thankful woman that John still mostly chooses to laugh instead of shoot me.

When we first got married, we were just figuring out how to have friends who were couples, too. I remember that whenever we would hang out with them, I would think, *Oh, she must be so lucky to be married to him. He's a great guy.* Then the more we would get to know them and the more I learned about the "great guy," the better John looked. So after a while, I started skipping the first step ("oh, she's so lucky") altogether and finally realized this truth: when it comes to marriage, none of us is a deal. We are all broken and flawed and come not only with baggage but also with a fully matched set and enough issues to fully stock the periodicals section of Barnes and Noble.

When my husband used to counsel engaged couples, he would take them through a prescribed curriculum that was supposed to help them live happily ever after through great communication. I thought it misleading to let them think this was the key element of a happy, long-lasting marriage. It is certainly an important element, but one that takes a long time to develop. By the time you actually begin to understand one another, you start tapering off on the total amount of communication. When you get to a certain point in your marriage, it is inevitable that you won't talk about stuff as much as you used to. This is because after discussing issues over and over and over and over and over and over and over again, you pretty much know exactly what the other person is going to say. After a while, you have done a sort of mental cartography; you have identified the landscape of your spouse's brain and you know where the peaks, valleys, rivers, and ruts reside. As much as I would like to believe that my man would love to know my opinion on any given subject, we are at the stage where, based on the last twenty-two years of history, he can pretty much figure it out without putting himself at risk by asking. It's sorta like verbal shorthand.

Strangely enough, this is usually the point in a marriage when many people decide that it must be over because "we don't talk anymore." I say that when you get to that point, rejoice! It means you have reached a new level of understanding. John and I now have new ways we make up for the loss of traditional forms of communication. We now have something akin to the way the great white whales communicate. It happens at night when we are lying in bed and have just settled in to drift off: suddenly, one of our stomachs will make a very nondescript noise. I think this is really interesting in that when I was younger, there was no stomach noise at all. My stomach did its work quietly and efficiently. With age and my acquired padding, you would think the sounds would be more muffled. *Au contraire, mon cher.* It seems the flab acts as an amplifier of sorts, and as my stomach sings its song, John's stomach will call out with an answer. This antiphonal digestive love song continues until one of the stomachs is exhausted and we are sore from laughing.

Communication in America really hasn't changed all that much over the past one hundred years, has it? We had the Native Americans getting their smoke signals messed up on windy days, the telegraph operators mixing up their dits and dashes, the switchboard operators giving you the wrong connection, and now we have arrived at the epitome of space-age connectivity: "Can you hear me now?"

Our whole family has cell phones. We wanted them so we could be in on the constant communication craze. Even John and I have things to say when we get on our cell phones—even though, as I said earlier, we pretty much already know everything that the other one is gonna say. We use them more as the epitome of laziness; I can call him when he's out in the yard and tell him that dinner is ready.

Cell phones are getting smaller and smaller, and I don't know if this is necessarily a good thing. They used to ring really loudly—and I mean the "ring" sound, not the four thousand annoying tunes you can download now. The smaller they get, the softer the sound gets. I can't tell you how many times I have been in the grocery store and someone's cell will start ringing. Immediately twenty-three women lift their purses up to their ears to see if it's theirs.

Anyway, the real problem with John's cell phone is this: unless I am with him to tell him it is ringing, he can't hear the thing. This would seem to defeat the whole purpose. I am hoping the cell phone companies will move beyond the "vibration" mode into "electroshock" mode.

Another thing about my husband is that he believes that just because he has read about a place or seen it on a map or ever met a person from that place, he is automatically qualified as a tour guide for that locale. It never ceases to amaze me that we will drive into a city we've never been to before and he will start pointing things out as if he grew up there. I used to actually be taken in by his tour-guide act, but now I know he is just making this stuff up. I am going to get him a hat that says, "Tour Guide for Places I've Never Been." If only he could drive as well as he makes that stuff up.

My dad taught me defensive driving (which would make all the other drivers on the road "offensive"). He was a government employee, and they were required to take defensive driving programs every so often to be qualified to drive vehicles from the motor pool. So the principles he taught me are firmly engrained in my driving psyche, principles like:

- "Follow at a distance of one car length for each ten miles per hour of speed to make sure you have room to stop."
- "Watch what the other drivers are doing, because you could be doing everything right and they still might hit you."
- "Always signal ahead of the time you are wanting to make your move in traffic. No one can read your mind."
- "Always be a courteous driver and let other people in if they ask you to."

I even feel so confident of my driving skills that I have started a little nonprofit business I like to call "Driver's Universal Counseling Service." As sole administrator of this community service, I spend my time behind the wheel helping instruct other drivers on how they should be driving. Unfortunately, none of them ever hears me or stops to ask me how I think their driving rates. I would be much more effective in my counseling if people would list their cell phone numbers right on their license plates. Then I could call them up and really assist them.

I am married to a man who is the definitive "offensive driver," and I don't mean that in the sense that he is offending people; he just thinks every run to the grocery store is like fourth and goal and that he must power through to the end zone.

In the past five years, he's gotten worse—or I've gotten more aware. Maybe both. Perhaps when I was younger, I was too busy replacing pacifiers in kids' mouths or unwrapping their Happy Meal toys to pay adequate attention. Whatever the case, his driving is a source of blood pressure elevation and adrenaline surge for me.

John actually believes he has some sort of superpowers. All men believe this about some area of their life. You might think your man is an exception, but I guarantee that you are just not paying close enough attention. John's area of superpower delusion is in the imaginary force field that he believes moves in front of our vehicle, something akin to a Cosmic Cow Pusher. For those of you not rural enough to know what a cow pusher is, it's that V-shaped thing that sticks out front of old-timey trains. This would push cows off the tracks so they wouldn't mess up the train wheels (gross). Anyway, John believes that by the mere force of his will he can continue accelerating (even though the car ahead has large red brake lights lighting up) and will be able to move this obstruction from his path with his Cosmic Cow Pusher. He also suffers from this delusion with regard to traffic lights; he believes that by continuing to accelerate, he can somehow force the light to change.

He does this to pedestrians as well. At the Kroger parking lot, they have that stripy section painted in the middle—the one that means, "This is where the people preoccupied with their groceries, carts, cell phones, and car keys are walking. Stop and let them be distracted without killing our customers, please." My husband likes to pull up to the edge of the stripes and keep rolling into the stripe area while motioning for the people to walk on across. This is very confusing for them, because they don't know if he is going to stop or just keep rolling and hit them. So they do the little "indecisi-jig"—you know, that little two-step dance you do when you don't know whether to step out or step back. John sees absolutely nothing wrong with keeping them guessing. So I just slink down in the truck seat and hope nobody recognizes us.

I did experience a moment of revelation one night when we were driving to Florida. It explained so much. John kept saying, "Did you see that deer? They're all over tonight." I never saw any of them. After the tenth time he said this, I responded, "How are you seeing all of them and I am seeing none of them?" He actually said, "I'm watching the ditches." Suddenly, I felt a wave of revelation sweep over me: *That explains everything. All this time I was under the impression that it was the driver's job to watch the road, but apparently, if you are male, you watch the ditch.*

He always points out to me that he hasn't killed us yet. Somehow this does not comfort me.

mother
superior

When John and I got married, I thought we needed to have ten kids—and right away. I may have had an "Olivia Walton" complex and thought that would make a really wonderful family model:

"'Night, Mary Ellen."

"'Night, John Boy."

Cue folksy music.

That was all fine and well until we had our first child and I came to know the meaning of the word "pain." There is a reason they call it "labor."

This was back during the time that Jane Fonda was doing her pregnancy workout videos and convincing everyone that natural childbirth was the intelligent choice. I believed her. I had all three of my children without an epidural and believed I was superior for it. When I consider it now, I believe I was just young. Childbirth was definitely not as simple as it was pictured in Jane Fonda's book. I thought the TV character of Murphy Brown came closer to reality when she was trying to explain childbirth to a male character: "Have you ever tried getting out of your car through the exhaust pipe?"

We had our first child, Calvin, when we were still finishing college. We lived in a tiny duplex for married students right across the football field from the college. We both had a semester left before graduation and we did what all young parents do when they have their first child: just went on as if nothing much had changed. We would put Calvin in our little backpack carrier and switch off between classes. Some days he would go to class with us. We were very blessed to have a fat, nap-loving baby, and he was as bored with the lectures as we were. So it was that Calvin went to college before he could walk.

As is the particular burden of firstborns, we believed that we would be the best parents that ever walked the earth. We did all the classic first-time parent stuff: too many pictures, too much sterilization of the pacifier, too many educational toys. I think we were secretly afraid we might in actuality be the *worst* parents ever, so we did all those things to prove to ourselves that we were doing all we could. This is why I believe that the Bible is only fair in its tradition of giving the firstborn the most stuff. Firstborns earn it.

With the additional attention firstborns receive, they also get the pressure to make us look good as parents. If they don't walk when they should, talk when they should, potty-train when they should, then there must be something wrong with our parenting skills. I remember consulting the "First Years" books to see what the "normal" range was for certain events. We were always thrilled when our child was earlier. Looking back now, I realize what a ridiculous exercise it was. Who cares if your kid is potty-trained six months earlier? Other than the fact that you get to save that much money on diapers, it's not normally an issue when they get ready to go to kindergarten. The pressure to perform is immense for firstborns, and that is precisely why most of them turn out to be type A overachieving neurotics. This is why they deserve the birthright.

Additional children don't get the majority of the inheritance, because they get born into a different family than the firstborn — usually a much more relaxed family. The secondborn's birthright is that the firstborn has already taken all the heat to do everything on time. Thus, the parents have decided that their parenting skills (or lack of) will probably not permanently maim or scar these resilient little people. Everybody exhales and the rest of the children are subsequently born into a more accepting, relaxed, and loving (if not germicidal) environment.

I've actually heard parents say, "I don't know how our kids could have turned out so differently from one another. We raised them both the exact same way." That's just not even remotely possible. With every child that comes into a family, the dynamics change. You might *think* you are the same person with each child, but that isn't possible, either. There is an ancient Indian proverb that says, "You can never step into the same river twice." The flow of the river constantly changes, and so it is with families.

Our three children are all so different from each other that John and I wonder how they came out of the same DNA pool at all. They are immeasurably different. For that, I am thankful. I haven't had the common temptation to compare them with each other.

Austin came into this world (three years after Calvin) ready to stand toe-to-toe with his brother and claim his space. I remember the day I was at the DMV to renew my license. Because we were living in a new state, I had to retake the test. Both the boys were in the room with me, and I was holding Austin (then a year old) while trying to scribble the little circles in with my pencil. Four-year-old Calvin kept reaching across the desk, and Austin would then move Calvin's arm off.

When I was done with the test, I stood up and handed it in. The DMV officer said to me, "Territorial, isn't he?" It never occurred to me that Austin was doing more than playing a game with his brother. But he was actually saying, "This space is mine, bub." That was the first time I realized that secondborns have to claim and protect anything they believe is theirs, as firstborns seem to have squatter's rights because they got there first. John and I have categorically rejected the traditional idea that the middle child gets treated unfairly. It was our belief that Austin had the primo spot in the family, as he could just as comfortably swing between his older brother's friends and his younger sister's friends. I'm not sure if he ever really bought into it, but he is the most versatile of our kids. He is also a loving, sensitive kid and tells people that he is a "teenage single parent." This is true, because he sponsors a Compassion International child in Tanzania.

Elyse came along three years later, and we were all glad to have a girl. I needed someone who would be willing to watch Lifetime Television with me. (Has anyone noticed that all the original programming on that station is about stalkers, switched-at-birth babies, surgical tragedies, and addictions? Maybe the channel could have been more realistically named "Things women hope never happen to them in their lifetime.") At least I *thought* Elyse was going to be my girlie TV buddy. Seems she grew up to love watching hockey (a most violent sport), and she gets really angry if they cut to commercial during a good fight. At least she likes to shop for shoes, so I wasn't a total failure.

When Elyse was born, we had the boys come up to the hospital room that night to get a look at the new kid on the block. We have them on video tiptoeing into the room. They came right up to the bed, where Elyse was lying across my lap, and looked at her for a few seconds in silence. Then Austin said, "Mommy, she's got a big head!" Okay, so he wasn't *always* loving and sensitive.

After Elyse was born, I felt that my "Olivia Walton" desires had been eclipsed by the realization that childbirth was not a stroll in the park and that I now had a permanent tired, achy feeling between my eyes. John and I prayed about it and decided our quiver was full. Now the reality of exactly what it takes to keep three kids well, well fed, and happy was setting in. I did find out one really interesting phenomenon, though. Did you know that you can sing *any* words you want to a child as long as you keep that breathy, lullaby voice? You can. This was wonderful for me because I could hone my songwriting skills while rocking my babies. I would use the tune of "Brahm's Lullaby" and sing stuff like:

> Go to sleep, go to sleep, go to sleep, Mom's exhausted
> I'm depressed, I need rest—just four hours in a row
> All my friends brag and say that their kid sleeps for hours
> I'd be proud if allowed just one five-minute shower

I don't fit in my jeans and my stretch marks need cream
Will these bags on my thighs ever shrink down in size?
When you're clean and pristine, you smell fresh just like clover
You're so cute 'til you poop and the smell knocks me over

When you pass a little gas, you smile just like your daddy
If you'll let me sleep 'til noon, I'll never make you clean your room
If I cope there's some hope you won't show up on Springer
I was wild as a child — now it's my turn to pay

If you are the mother of a baby or young toddler, try it. They don't know what you're saying.

I've heard my friend say that when her four children were less than five years old, some afternoons she would climb into the playpen so that the kids couldn't get her for a while. They were perfectly content to play all around her (they could still see her) and she would lie there quietly. As they don't make play-pens as sturdy as they used to, I wouldn't recommend it now. Sounds like the directions on the aspirin bottle: "Take two. Keep away from children." Or perhaps moms of toddlers could have a warning tattooed on their foreheads like those aerosol cans do: "Contents under pressure."

One thing that really gets the hair up on my neck is when I hear these newfangled parents asking for their children's approval all the time. You've heard it, too. It's like they have to punctuate every sentence they speak to their child (no matter how young) with the question, "Okay?"

"We're going to the bank now, okay?"

"We can't have that toy now, okay?"

"The doctor is going to give you a little vaccination shot, okay?"

Well of course it isn't going to be "okay" with that child—and then where do you stand? As if your decision was going to be swayed by the child's approval. As far as I can tell, that actually makes it a lie because you are not going to change your actions just because your child says it's not okay with him or her. What a huge responsibility to place on a four-year-old, having to "okay" everything all the time. And if the child doesn't "okay" whatever it is, doesn't that then make the mother disrespectful of the child's wishes? And doesn't this put the child at the very pinnacle of the decision-making processes of the household? How unfair is that? A child is supposed to feel loved and cared for and safe. How safe can the world be if a four-year-old must "sign off" on all that the adults do?

Okay, off my personal soapbox.

I thought we were a real family when we had our first child. But basically your first child is an accessory for your marriage. It might slow your roll a little, but you can pretty much take the offspring with you. You will look cute together. That first child is like a hood ornament for your marital union. With the second child comes the new wave of laundry and you are now officially tired *and* on duty 24/7. With the third child, there are now more of them than there are adults, so you have to switch from man-to-man to more of a zone defense. And it is much like herding cats: a lot of effort for not much formation. This was also when the concept of "team effort" really crystallized for me. It now meant that everyone on the "team" needed to be giving maximum "effort" to get done whatever I said.

No matter how many books you read or classes you attend, almost all of parenthood is on-the-job training. I can tell you some of the stuff I learned, though. I learned that if you need to hide a birthday or Christmas present from a child, you can stick it in the dishwasher. No child ever looks in there for anything. (You can apply the same principle for husbands. It seems that there is some sort of force field that makes things invisible to the male eye if you place the item directly behind the milk on the top shelf of the refrigerator.) I learned that no matter what any beautiful brochure tells you about a vacation spot, absolutely *nothing* is fun for the *whole* family. Write it down: someone will suffer.

My kids also learned quickly. They learned that if you wanted to sneak something on Mom, you didn't have to get up very early in the morning, because I didn't get up very early in the morning. I've always been a late-night kind of girl, and a lot of people told me that when I had kids, that would have to change. I never really got that whole thing. Until the kids were school-age, I just let them stay up with me, and then they would sleep longer in the morning. Not a problem. By the time they were school-age, they could get their own cereal in the morning. Sometimes I wake up early and hear all the birds singing so sweetly — and *loudly*. I think to myself, *Can't you guys just knock it off for another hour?*

Morning is just plain overrated. I know, I know — there are all those Scriptures about seeking the Lord early in the morning, and all you morning people always beat us night people up about it. But if I am having my time with God at 1 or 2 AM, aren't I (technically) beating you to it?

Morning people are so chipper and annoying. They will call you up at some awful hour (like 8:30) and chirp into the phone, "Oh, did I wake you?" as if they can't tell. They know good and well that they woke you. They planned to do it, and then they spend the next fifteen minutes telling you everything they've accomplished while you were sleeping: "I got up at 4:30 and had the most amazing Bible study and prayer time. Then I knit a sweater for my nephew for Christmas. Then I repotted all my roses, had a four-course breakfast, showered, and thought I'd ring you up to see what you're going to do today," like maybe they are looking for ideas after running out of their own. I say START THE DAY LATER, and then you won't have to look for so much stuff to fill it up. And have you ever noticed there are millions of postcards with sunsets on them and *none* with sunrises on them? I rest my case. Back to the subject of offspring.

I love our kids. They have been a great source of continual joy for us. Every age has had its particular challenges but also so much delight. Because our kids are in their late teens to early twenties now, we are in the midst of learning how to help them launch into adulthood. It is a wonder to us how God gives you these little people to love and nurture and then they turn into these wonderful adults you would love to hang around with even if they weren't yours.

One night we were asked to bring our kids (then ages sixteen, thirteen, and nine) to a parenting Bible study so that the small group could ask our kids about how we had raised them and then ask us questions separately. I was immediately filled with conflicting emotions of pride and terror—pride because our friends thought we had done such a good job in our child rearing, and terror because of the things our kids could tell this group of adults.

Although I protested that it might be a little early to say that we had done a good job (they weren't all grown — who knew if they would need long-term adult therapy?), I was inwardly feeling pret-ty good about the whole thing. So that night, I decided I would wear my black leather jacket and my black leather mules so that I would have the Maximum Cool Mom Effect. Right as we drove up into their driveway, it started to rain. Wanting to protect my leather, I decided to make a run for the porch. Fine, except I am not too coordinated and my mules decided to go one direction as my feet went another. I went down in a spastic flail and ripped open my slacks, shredded the skin on my knee, and hit the side of my head. My children were not so much filled with compassion as they were trying not to snort when they laughed.

So much for Miss Cool Mom.

I don't think I always made such great decisions when raising my kids. I remember one time when Elyse was a baby and we had only one car. John was at the church and I had decided to do like all the other moms in my neighborhood and take my children out for fresh air. I believe it was a few weeks after Christmas because Calvin had a brand-new scooter and Austin had a Big Wheel trike. Calvin must have been six, Austin three, and Elyse just a couple of months old.

Calvin had been asking me to take him down the street so he could ride somewhere besides our driveway. We had made it about three blocks from our home when a neighbor boy rode up on a brand-new bike. He was about the same age as Calvin, and the dude was obviously proud of his new ride. "Wanna race, Calvin?"

he asked my son. Calvin looked at the downhill cul-de-sac, with its steep grade, and looked at me to give him motherly wisdom. Did I counsel him to think twice because of his inexperience? Did I tell him that I thought it wouldn't be advisable because the hill was steep and the other boy had a bigger ride? No. These are the things a *good* mother would say. I, however, distinctly remember saying, "I think you can take him."

Calvin looked down the hill and back at me. I gave him the thumbs up. I even said, "On your mark, set, go!"

The rest, as they say, is Emergency Room history.

Calvin did, indeed, beat the bigger kid on the bike. But because he had only ridden in our driveway and around our yard, he had no experience with the speed you pick up going downhill. So once he got to the bottom of that cul-de-sac, he was going faster than he ever had before. He looked up and saw a mailbox coming at him and abandoned the scooter only to fall into the gravel that was lining the pavement, cleanly slicing his knee. Here I was at the top of this cul-de-sac with a newborn and a three-year-old on a Big Wheel and my six-year-old was now panicking. I have no idea how I got them all down the hill and back up again (I've heard that you can do miraculous things due to adrenaline), but John came home and took us to the ER for a little knee repair on my firstborn, thus ending Calvin's racing career and beginning my eradication of certain phrases from my motherhood vocabulary including, "I think you can take him."

You probably know the saying "You'd better be nice to your kids. They're gonna choose your nursing home one day." It used to be such a bad thing when they had to "put you in" The Home. People used to treat their grown children better than they deserved for fear they would be put into a bad Home. Thanks to shows like *60 Minutes* (which always seems longer than that, doesn't it?), which has done exposé pieces on the atrocious living conditions in some of those facilities, we now have something like a resort to send the older folks to when they no longer are able to do for themselves. They call these "assisted-living homes" and they're like halfway houses for old folks. You don't have to go *all the way* into a nursing home; you can just be "assisted."

These places have fabulous amenities. You can live in your own little apartment, have access to all the transportation you want, have your doctor come visit you (just for fun: have your activities director ask the doctor to take off *his* clothes, put on a thin gown, and wait outside *your* room for a while), and have three meals per day that you choose from a varied menu. Maids come in and clean your room. The activities director plans trips and socials for all of the ladies spry enough to have an eye on one of the gentlemen. Some of these assisted-living homes have beauticians on site and high-speed Internet connections. Some of them even have luxuries like masseuses and turndown service at night. My daughter volunteers at one near us, and after visiting over there with her I am trying to figure out exactly how old you must be before you can check in.

I think I might want to go there while I am still young enough to enjoy it. I'll just call up my kids and say, "Mom wants to go to the assisted-living home now, okay?"

the art and craft of doing nothing

S ome of you will appreciate my newfound area of excellence: doing nothing and resting afterward. It flies in the face of the Puritan work ethic we've all been taught and feels more decadent than a five-pound box of Godiva chocolates all to yourself. I would love to start a new habit amongst us perpetually tired women: ritualized resting.

Doesn't it seem that Sunday afternoons were specially made for napping? The equation I use to determine the success of a nap is the amount of drool that is created multiplied by the depth of the pillow line on my face. Some of us who really love to sleep actually dream about napping. I've always felt cheated that we live in a country that doesn't embrace the afternoon siesta.

Another activity that's an exquisite joy all its own is bathing. Many of us are already ritual bathers. How else can you explain the proliferation of bath and body shops? I have bath products for every conceivable mood. There are scents for calming, energizing, unstuffing sinuses, inspiring romance, and relieving stress. I've got loofahs and scrubbies and sponges and pillows and pumice stones. My bathtub is lined with candles, and I have a setting on my iPod called "Bath Time" with my favorite downtime songs loaded. John got this iPod for me for Christmas (I only begged and begged for it!). It has the smallest amount of memory iPod offers (ten gigabytes), and it still holds about 2,500 songs. It is conceivable that aside from being caught in elevators, getting put on hold, or attending weddings or funerals, I never *ever* have to listen to a song I don't like for the rest of my life. How great is that?

As Sylvia Plath says in her novel *The Bell Jar*, "There may be some things that a hot bath won't cure, but I don't know of any." I have entered the time of my life when the crowning achievement of any given day is whether or not I can get home, get a hot bath in my own tub, and get into my own bed. I remember listening to my grandmother and her old neighbor women speak of this ritual as if it were sacred. I listened to them talk about it during the time in my life (ages four to twelve) when the most reviled part of my day had to do with bathing and going to sleep. I thought to myself, *That is the definition of elderly: the desire to bathe and go to sleep in your own bed.* I imagined nothing more glamorous than having the option to travel the world, skip the bath, and stay up all night should I so choose.

I am now officially "elderly."

I will not, however, bathe in hotels. This is mostly because I don't know who was in there last and whether the hotel maid was thorough. And is there a level of "thorough enough" when it comes to a bathtub? I will shower in a hotel, but never bathe. Eeeew.

I don't sleep well in hotel rooms either. This has everything to do with the fact that hotels have not discovered the modern invention called "fitted sheets." Consequently, after the second turn in the bed, two of the four corners have come untucked and all wrinkled up. You are now filling for the "sheet burrito," and there is nothing worse than trying to sleep on a pile of wrinkles.

I can't tell you how many times over the past year that the thought of getting home to my own bath and bed has kept me from losing my brain on the plane ride home. When we are still on the tarmac an hour after boarding and are now thirty-fifth in line on the runway for takeoff, I simply keep chanting, "I will be in my own tub in less than six hours, I will be in my own bed in less than seven hours." And I regain composure and perspective.

Before my husband came on the road with me, he realized the necessity of that restorative bath in my life. He would have me call him when I was ten minutes from the house so that he could start the bathwater, light some candles around the ledge of the tub, and place some grapes and chocolate within reach. (I know, I know—your man does not do this for you, right? You know what I say to that? "Train up a man in the way that he should go.") John knows that the moment I step into that tub, I instantly morph from "Grubby Gripe-y Girl" to "Happy to Be Home Girl," all due to the power of the lowly bathtub.

And soft sleeping clothes? Another necessity. For some, it's pj's. For some, it's gowns. For some, T-shirts are the best-feeling option. Whatever your design issues, softness is a nonnegotiable. And you need soft sheets (the higher the thread count, the closer to heaven).

I love that the Bible tells us that God didn't create Sabbath for Himself but that it was a life principle that we human beings were desperately in need of. It seems that one of the most difficult things to do is to truly cease from all of our efforts and then relax and enjoy our life apart from the work of it. With the advent of laptops and cell phones, it is now entirely possible to never leave work. Those of us who work at home know the particular temptation to get up at night and try to cram a little more work into the twenty-four hours.

I'm thinking that God didn't rest after Creation because it really tuckered Him out. He merely spoke and things came to be. No, God knew that if He didn't model rest for us, we wouldn't get it. So He did. He worked, and then He rested.

For many of us, resting does not come easily. We feel unworthy if we are not "pulling our weight." But any farmer worth his salt knows that you can't plow with the same oxen more than six hours at a time. The beasts need rest. The farmer also knows that if you continue to plant a field season after season and never allow it to go fallow and replenish its nutrients, the harvest will be weak. There are certain seasons when even dirt is supposed to be left alone and barren in order to rejuvenate and be fertile for the next seven years.

Most of us have experienced a form of Christianity that implies that if you are not constantly moving forward, then there must be something wrong with you. What about the fallow times? Isn't it possible that in every life there must come a time when the ground is not producing but is still so that it might be even more fruitful at a later time? Maybe we've stripped the field of life by continuing to attempt a harvest when it's time to just be fallow.

If working is so hard, planning to rest is harder. It's difficult to do nothing. If it were easy, God wouldn't have had to give so many rules to the Israelites about what they could and could not do on the day of rest. If you doubt that this is true, I challenge you to start taking a day once a week to truly rest and appreciate the life God has given you. It is difficult for us to admit that we need it, but a once-a-week "unplugging" from the frenetic pace that is now our norm can be one of the most spiritually liberating experiences for us and for our family.

Part of this resting is the activity that God modeled for us when He rested from His creative labors and declared that "it is good" (see Genesis 1). We definitely need to take the time to love and appreciate all the good that is in our lives and declare it to be so.

King Solomon wisely declared,

> I know that there is nothing better for men than to be happy and do good while they live. That everyone may eat and drink, and find satisfaction in all his toil—this is the gift of God. I know that everything God does will endure forever; nothing can be added to it and nothing taken from it. God does it so that men will revere him. (Ecclesiastes 3:12-14)

Some of us need to declare our efforts in the prior days of our workweek "good!" and give ourselves a little pat on the back. We might need to look around and declare that our spouse is "good!" and tell him so, or maybe our children. They need to hear that you consider them "good" in your life. Our families are not our projects for us to manage; they are gifts from God to be enjoyed. Wouldn't it be a kick to just enjoy our lives for one day out of seven instead of spending all our energy trying to fix and improve it?

In order to welcome "ritual" resting into your life, you need to recognize your need for it, plan for it, be fully present in it, and protect it. When we are at rest, we can cut through the noise of the urgent to hear the call of the important. We have time to think about the things that make life sweet. We are restored in our faith to live our lives authentically and powerfully.

Remember this: it's impossible to tap dance for the world while soaking in a sudsy tub.

bible
babes

I'm a math idiot. I got lost somewhere in third grade when we started on long division. All that carrying and lining up the numbers to subtract made me tired. The abacus was supposed to make it clearer somehow, but I couldn't get past the cool way the beads clinked when you pushed them together.

I got completely left behind with the whole fractions deal. (It was only in college when someone explained that it was like money that the lightbulb came on for me.) When I made it to eighth grade and they started in with the pre-algebra, they might as well have been speaking in that voice the teacher in the Peanuts cartoon used: "Woenk woenk woenk woenk woenk." I couldn't project ahead and find a single future scenario where I would possibly need to know the value of x. I can, however, calculate down to the cent how much a $79.98 jacket would be at 70 percent off. This ability is my most savant-like talent.

But being a math idiot, I can't begin to think of the equation that would produce an accurate estimate of how many sermons I have heard in my lifetime—not just once on Sunday mornings and evenings (sometimes we had multiple morning services and, being the piano player, I had to ride the bus twice) but intermittent revivals and conferences. This would definitely take algebra. There are a handful of Sunday sermons that stand out, however.

We once had a pastor who would take out his cotton handkerchief while onstage and blow his nose—and I mean really honk on it. He would then open the handkerchief and examine the contents. (*What* was he looking for? Rubies and diamonds?) He stood there and did it in the pulpit without even acknowledging the muffled gagging sound rippling through the pews.

Another Sunday that stands out for me was in a different church, where the pastor was preaching on those times throughout biblical history when God intervened in ways that only He could. The pastor went on to say that there are many times in the Bible when man is in an impossible situation and nothing can be done, and the situation only turns around when we read the words "but God." It would have been fine if he'd stopped there, but he felt the need to explain that those "buts" were "very *big* buts." I'm not sure if he understood why people had their heads down and were shaking while trying to contain their laughter. I thought it would be a great idea for him to write a devotional book called *The Really Big Buts of the Bible.*

In all those sermons, I never once heard a pastor or teacher say they had trouble with certain verses. They always had their arsenal of commentaries to help them with the various difficult passages. Goody for them.

Now, I know that the Bible is a complex book (actually, a collection of many smaller books). Some of the books are historical, while others are of wisdom and poetry. Some are accounts of the life and ministry of Jesus, and some are letters from Paul attempting to encourage his missionaries. The love of God for us is evident throughout Scripture. But I also would argue that there are parts of the Bible that are harder to put into practice than others.

Thomas Jefferson seemed to have had the same problem, although he took the solution a little too far by creating his own bible. He would take the parts of the Bible that he didn't agree with and cut them out. I wonder if his pages were printed on both sides. If so, what happened if a part that he *did* agree with was on the other side? You know, like when you're cutting coupons out of a magazine and there's a great article on the other side.

I don't want to actually remove anything from the Bible; there are just some Scriptures that I've found harder to practice than others. For instance:

"Therefore I tell you, do not worry about your life, what you will eat or drink; or about your body, what you will wear." (Matthew 6:25)

I ask every woman, why did *that* one have to be in the Bible? Why, oh, why?

That one is harder to obey than all the Ten Commandments put together. I don't know *any* female (not in a coma) who can go thirty minutes without transgressing that particular one. And it would be hard if Jesus had said only that we aren't supposed to think about what we are going to eat (isn't this fully 50 percent of our waking time?), but then He follows it up with the wardrobe issue! It takes up major frontal lobe space because we are either wondering what we are going to wear to our next place, regretting what we already have on, or thinking about the next purchase that will make our lives complete.

Wives, submit to your husbands. (Ephesians 5:22)

This is a tough one. It's not that I disagree with the principle, as in verse 21 Paul tells everyone that we should all submit to each other. It's just that in verse 22, he tells wives specifically. The husbands only get the command, "Love your wives." I ask you, how hard can this be, seeing as how we are all so totally loveable? This concept of submission to my husband used to be a little easier back when we first got married. He was the big and strong man, and I weighed less. Now that I'm a little bigger than I was back in the day, it's much harder to submit, because I'm fairly sure that I could take him.

And even though the Bible says we are to submit, I don't think that means we're not supposed to raise objections (sometimes loudly and with tears). But let's face it: someone has to be the one to make the final decision.

Let me just save you a lot of time, girls. Let your man do it. Here's why. Do you know *why* men get married? It's not the cooking and cleaning (they could pay for that). They get married (ultimately) so they will have someone to blame stuff on. You don't believe me? Exhibit A: the first man ever created, "Lord, it was that woman you gave to me who made me do it!"

Hey, if the tendency to blame the wife goes all the way back to the Garden of Eden, it's a done deal. When God said He was going to whip up a suitable helpmate, He may have been thinking of all the help that man would need to think things through. A friend of mine says that when he and his wife got married, they vowed that he would be the one to make all of the important decisions in the marriage. He reports that they have yet to make even one important decision. So be forewarned: if you don't want to hear about how your way didn't work out and get it thrown in your face for the next forty years of marriage, it's better to just let him handle it so he can't blame it on you.

"Love your enemies." (Matthew 5:44)

I could really get on the bandwagon called "tolerance" here. As a rule, I think the whole tolerance thing is overdone, as if merely learning to peaceably coexist is going to transport us to cultural nirvana. Tolerance is learning to live with something you can't change. I have learned to tolerate sweltering summers in the South. I tolerate restaurants that don't serve sweet tea. I tolerate perimenopause. Unfortunately, Jesus didn't ask me to merely tolerate my enemies. And I could really excel in tolerance. I could allow my enemies to occupy my world all the livelong day, as long as I don't have to interact with them. In the story of the good

Samaritan, the priest and the Levite "tolerated" the beaten man by allowing him to coexist on their road. But tolerance wasn't Jesus' point. He asked for something much more: love. This kind of love is proactive and compels me to reach beyond noticing a bundle of behaviors to see deep inside a human soul. Only God's love could make that feat possible.

"If you do not forgive men their sins, your Father will not forgive your sins." (Matthew 6:15)

This does not sound like the easy grace I was taught as a young'un. In my flannelgraph Sunday-school world, God was love and forgiveness, and all you had to do was confess your sins and you would be forgiven. There was none of this conditional stuff being discussed back then. I can't recall the first time I read this verse in context, but I remember being shocked that there was an instance given where God would not forgive me. This rocked my world! This was like somebody remembering to read the rules in the middle of the game. But there it is, hanging out there from the lips of Jesus. It seems I'm controlling the valve that allows the flow of forgiveness in my life. I don't think I like having that kind of power. Gulp.

Rejoice in the Lord *always*. (Philippians 4:4)
Give thanks in *all* circumstances.
(1 Thessalonians 5:18)

Do not be anxious about *any*thing.
  (Philippians 4:6)
I can do *every*thing through [Christ].
  (Philippians 4:13)
In *all* things God works for the good of those who
    love him. (Romans 8:28)

I put these Scriptures all in one lump because they are all-inclusive. I call them the "no excuses" verses. These are the ones that totally bust me when it comes to my whining and rationalizing. The unfortunate part of these being in the Bible is that they take me to task whenever I feel as if there is some situation too difficult for me to maintain a heart of gratitude. If Paul had only said, "Do not be anxious about *most* things," we could have had a little more latitude with the attitude. Whaa!

It seems to me that in all those bazillion sermons I have listened to, I would be so biblically knowledgeable and truth-imbued that I could follow Christ with one brain tied behind my back. But it doesn't work that way. The more you know about the Bible, the more convinced you become that you haven't scratched the surface of its depth. That's why we have all sorts of Bible studies going on everywhere, all the time.

While I think of the Bible as a book meant to be enjoyed and treasured, some like to treasure it with methodical studies, outlines, essays, and fill-in-the-blanks. When those I consider "Bible Babes" know exactly where to find what they're looking for *without* the assistance of a concordance, I am truly awe-inspired at their memorization and devotion. There are many times I have had to say, "It's in there somewhere," and then do a "search" function on my Bible software to find out where the "somewhere" actually is.

We've got all sorts of Bible-study workbooks and notebooks and study guides and videos and retreats and conferences and seminars. With all of these cool resources at our disposal, I still find that you can mine a lot of great theology from unlikely sources. You have to do some of your own creative application, but it works. For example, because I like to troll the fridge in my house and even other people's houses (you'd be surprised that you can learn more about people from what's in their fridge than what's in their medicine cabinet—you should try it!), I sometimes gain great spiritual tidbits from refrigerator magnets. It's true. Next time you are standing and staring at your friend's refrigerator, just try and make a spiritual application from those magnets. It's like doing those midsection tightening exercises while standing in line at the bank: no one will know you are doing it, and eventually you'll be stronger for it.

If you really contemplate what some of those magnets say, you can carry off some invaluable nuggets of truth. I'll even get you started.

"No coffee, no workee."

This one is on my fridge. The spiritual application might be that without proper fuel, we're not gonna get very far in our "workee." That fuel may be the power of the Holy Spirit infusing our efforts, or the hookup to our life source, Jesus Christ. He said, "Apart from me you can do nothing" (John 15:5).

"A clean house is the sign of a boring woman."

Not on my fridge, but this is one that could be. If it's true, I must be the most interesting woman alive today. The biblical application might be from the story of Mary and Martha, where Martha was bustling about, making sure that all the stuff was taken care of, while her sister was enjoying Jesus (see Luke 10:38-42). I only hope that I could have the wisdom to know when it's time to go on a cleaning tear and when it's time to sit for a while with the Lord.

"Countless number of people have eaten in this kitchen and gone on to lead normal lives."

Don't our kids need to see this one? It's a great idea to give our daily situations the one-year/five-year/hundred-year test ("Will this matter in a year, five years, a hundred years?"). Over and over we read in the Bible, "and it came to pass." Perspective releases some of the air out of our overpressurized tires.

"You can't please everybody, so just concentrate on me."

My personal mantra to my husband! But it's true—we *can't* please everybody, especially when it comes to what to make for dinner. Most of the time, I am just internally conflicted enough to wonder if I'm even pleasing myself! So I've got to decide whose opinion is going to count the most. Man? Mom? Kid? Boss? I believe that this magnet is a great paraphrase of about 25 percent of the Bible. In this case, God is the Capital Me, aka "I Am" (Exodus 3:14).

"Hand over the chocolate and no one gets hurt."

This one reminds me that it might be a good idea to recognize my frustrations before they get to the point of violence. Proverbs 29:11 tells us, "A fool gives full vent to his anger, but a wise man keeps himself under control." Do I really want my family to remember me as the Out of Control Freak? Attitude check, please.

The Footprints Poem

I won't quote the poem here, but it has been a resident on many a fridge magnet. That poem speaks to us of God's mercy during a difficult time and how even when we no longer have strength, He will carry us.

I have come across another version of this poem, which I believe deserves equal fridge-time with the original version. This one speaks of how God does indeed expect that we will someday walk again.

BUTTPRINTS IN THE SAND

One night I had a wondrous dream
One set of footprints there was seen
The footprints of my precious Lord
But mine were not along the shore

But then some stranger prints appeared
And I asked the Lord, "What have we here?
Those prints are large and round and neat
But Lord, they are too big for feet."

"My child," He said in somber tones
"For miles I carried you alone
I challenged you to walk in faith
But you refused and made me wait

"You disobeyed, you would not grow
The walk of faith you would not know
So I got tired and got fed up
And there I dropped you on your butt

"Because in life there comes a time
When one must fight and one must climb
When one must rise and take a stand
Or leave their buttprints in the sand"

Author unknown. Accessed at www.pastornet.net.au/jmm/articles/12425.htm on June 22, 2004.

Wouldn't you like to give your whiny friends a framed copy of *that*?

But (and that's a big but) the Bible is as clear on the long-suffering and compassionate nature of God. He is patient with us and carries us so many more times than we may ever know. I just want to be ready for the time when He invites me to walk again.

So always be ready to find the nuggets of spiritual truth off the beaten path, because Bible Babes aren't *born*—they're *made*.

excess
baggage

When people ask me where I live, my response is that my address is an Atlanta suburb but it seems like I spend most of my time at the Atlanta airport baggage claim. As my travel schedule continues to expand, I spend a lot of time watching the bags go 'round and 'round.

It's amusing to watch people jockey for position right up on the luggage carousel and stare intently at the bags coming off the conveyor belt because they are of the belief that someone wants to steal their stuff. It's funny to me because the truth is, nobody wants *your* stuff. They only want *their* stuff. But we are so convinced that someone is gonna take *our* stuff and that then we might end up with *their* stuff, or worse, *no* stuff! And then we'll have to go out and buy *new* stuff, which, by the way, would be my definition of a really great day. Unfortunately, I always get my same old stuff.

I don't think I took an airplane trip until I was thirteen years old. But I got my first set of luggage when I was ten. It consisted of seven vinyl matching pieces that stacked inside each other. My grandmother bought them for me from the Montgomery Ward catalog, and I thought I was just somethin'. This was back in the day when you could have checked seven matching bags and you would have been thought of as stylish, not excessive—much less against FAA regulation. Prior to 1980, the luggage industry loved variety. They made plaids, tapestries, nubby wools, vinyl colors, and tough hardsides. One company even had that commercial showing its suitcase in a zoo cage with a gorilla throwing it all around and jumping up and down on it to simulate baggage handler conditions. They weren't far off base.

Somewhere between 1984 and 1996, the luggage industry lost its grip on reality and started manufacturing black bags only. Lots of people were mistakenly picking up the wrong bags and arriving at the hotel only to find that (horrors!) they had someone else's stuff. This was the genesis of BCP (Baggage Carousel Paranoia).

In talking to other frequent flyers, my experience has led me to believe that there is a great divide on the whole baggage issue and you fall into one of two distinct camps: you are either a Less Is Better traveler or a More Is Mo' Better traveler.

If you are in the Less Camp, you believe with all your widdle heart that you are superior because you can get everything you need into a carry-on bag. Your packing mantras?

- "Less is more."
- "Travel light."
- "When in doubt, leave it out."

You rejoice in your rolled-up suiting. You revel in your micro-travel-sized toiletries. You scoff at the people who check multiple bags. You feel pious pity for those who must tip a skycap.

If you are in the Mo' Better Camp, you believe with all your widdle heart that should *any* wardrobe opportunity present itself, you will be prepared to meet the challenge. You take the Boy Scout motto seriously. Besides, how can one possibly know ahead of time how one will *feel* on any given day? And if you dress according to your feelings, you must adequately prepare for a diverse emotional landscape. You need options, lots and lots of options! Your packing mantras?

- "Less is frightening."
- "Travel right."
- "When in doubt, take one in every color."

I am a Mo' Better girl myself. I don't dress to try to convey a certain message about myself as much as I dress to reflect how I am feeling on any given day. If I'm feeling bright and cheery, I'll be wearing something with High Cute Quotient. Melancholy? I'll be in something blue. Rowdy? Hand me my denim Harley jacket. Slightly sassy? I'd be needing my red patent leather cowboy boots with the white star on the front *and* the back (entrance *and* exit statement). So you can see how the suitcase would be dangerously near weight limit even before I start adding the shoes.

I also can't quite get the hang of paring down the toiletries to a manageable size. I'm always experimenting with different makeups and face creams and vitamins and hair products. I try to prepare for all sorts of skin emergencies (Will my skin be dry? Break out? Will I need sunscreen? Chapstick? Visine? Will I need to tweeze my eyebrows? Clean my ears out with Q-tips? Will I need Band-Aids? Hydrogen peroxide? Catgut suture?). And the older I get, the more putty and Spackle I need with me. I do not exaggerate when I say that I now travel with four different products that are designed specifically to "erase under-eye circles."

Now the airlines are limiting the number of bags you can check and actually charging for overweight bags. My husband has been forced to stand at the baggage counter while I juggle stuff between bags to get them all under the non-paying weight. He now puts them on the bathroom scale before we leave for the airport. Smart man.

The real challenge for me is trying not to look too spastic while getting my stuff from the car to the plane. I never feel like I am totally in control of this unwieldy wheeled mass. I try stacking things on top of each other and strapping them together, and I still end up feeling like I am "careening on" instead of "carrying on." And what about that announcement they make over the loudspeaker: "Do not accept or carry anything from any unknown or suspicious person." Is there really any possibility that I might have any openings to carry even one more item from *anybody*?

All the huffing and puffing gets me to the plane, where I must now force-fit the carry-on into the overhead bin. I have a very real fear of hoisting my bag into midair, only to realize that it is much too heavy for me to complete this dead lift, thus experiencing the gravity of having it brought down squarely on the head of the Passenger with a Highly Litigious Lawyer Friend. Once it is properly stowed (airlines are big on this concept), I can spend the next couple of hours trying to find a head position that doesn't crick my neck or allow me to drool should I nod off.

I wish I were better at the packing/traveling light gig. I think it's my insecurities that keep me piling the stuff in. Will I have enough? Have I covered every eventuality? Will I be caught without something I really need? Will there be a 24-Hour Super Target where I'm going?

And my life is like that. I spend too much time accumulating stuff that is supposed to ward off regrets. Instead, it makes me a terribly encumbered traveler, ever hoisting my junk from one phase of life to the next. I'm not sure if it's more difficult to keep from acquiring too much stuff or to let go of the stuff I no longer need. And when it comes to emotional baggage, I think we all come with fully matched sets.

I love what Jesus said about traveling with Him: "Are you tired? Worn out? Burned out on religion? Come to me. Get away with me and you'll recover your life. I'll show you how to take a real rest. Walk with me and work with me—watch how I do it. Learn the unforced rhythms of grace. I won't lay anything heavy or ill-fitting on you. Keep company with me and you'll learn to live freely and lightly" (Matthew 11:28-30, MSG).

Freely and lightly—sounds like a great invitation to exchange the baggage carousel for the one that comes standard with music, pretty horses, and wind in the face. No carry-ons allowed.

fully clothed and
not in my
right mind

Getting dressed isn't as easy as it used to be. My requirement used to be, "How cute could I look in this?" Now I am interested not so much in style as in clothing that doubles as gravity-defying architecture. This is my launch-from-closet checklist:

- Can I get out of it quickly should the "gotta go, gotta go, gotta go right now" urge hit? Check.
- Does it have elastic in the waist for the ever-changing middle? Check.
- Does it camouflage my flaws and accentuate the positive? Too much to ask from a single garment.
- Does it lift and separate? Check.
- Does it accommodate my voluptuous features without spillage? Check.
- When I sit, will it pinch? Check.

I usually end with, "Houston, we have a problem."

I now believe that when Jesus spoke some of His famous words, He must have looked down through time and known they would mean far more than they did back then. For instance, the verse that says, "When thou prayest, enter into thy closet" (Matthew 6:6, KJV). He had to know that if there were ever a time when I am faced with my utter human failings, it is when I go into my closet.

Maybe your closet is a testament to great organizational skills. If so, you cannot be my friend. But I ask you, how organized can your closet be when you are trying to hold on to five different sizes of clothes? You know what I mean. Every woman has The Largest Size I Will Allow, followed closely by the I Feel Fat but Not That Big, and the These Mostly Fit, hemmed in by the When I Lose Ten Pounds, and finished off with the Only If I Get My Jaw Wired Shut collection. And if your closet is anything like mine, it consists of about twelve inches of clothes you actually wear hopelessly squished by the eight feet of mistakes you cannot bear to part with because you paid too much for them. My closet is not so much a place where I keep my clothes as it is a museum of my shopping mistakes.

Whenever I do get the urge to purge my closet, I have difficulty thinking of people I like well enough to give these expensive mistakes. These lapses of judgment represent a streak of strident optimism (Sure, I can drop enough weight to let me squeeze into that! I defy all conventional color charts, which would say that I can't wear bright orange! Horizontal stripes? No problem!) and a significant financial outlay, wrong as it may be. I can't give them to just *anybody*. You know what I mean. There are certain friends or relatives who might enjoy wearing them, but you know that they don't properly separate their wash loads or check to see if an item is "dry-clean only." You would trust them to water your plants but not to take proper care of your fashion mistakes. These clothes are now like pets, and you want to make sure they find the right home.

So assuming I could wiggle myself into the closet, I would most definitely feel led to pray for myself and my wretched condition: my disorganization, my mistakes I can't let go of, my lack of self-discipline. That Scripture about going into the closet was dead-on.

I used to go into my closet to get dressed. I can't remember why this started. Maybe I just wanted to emerge in my outfit for a more dramatic effect. Not anymore. I can no longer pull my pantyhose on in the closet like I used to do. I used to just pull my knee up toward my chest and pull those things on in a flash. Now it seems I have to get in three very advanced yoga positions just to get them to a place where I can work them up. This takes way more space than my closet allows. Once I do get all that spandex and nylon wrangled onto my body, I am instantly aware that the label "control top" is a misnomer. It is not "controlling" anything; it is merely displacing it.

Maybe I'm not the only one who cleans out my closet just to avoid doing something else. As I am moving toward some kind of massive deadline, suddenly my closet starts calling out to me, "Organize me! Clean me out! Rid me of clutter!" Funny that I never hear it calling to me at any other time. But who said that being the Queen of Avoidance would be without complications?

When it's time to organize my closet, I have trouble staying on task. I start out with the best of intentions and end up spending only about ten minutes doing what I am supposed to be doing. I start by moving about ten things around in the closet, and then I realize that I have to go to the bathroom. While in there, I notice that the bathroom countertop is a mess. This leads to sharpening all the makeup pencils, which leads to dumping out the bathroom trash, which leads to deciding that I've never really liked that trash can anyway, which makes me decide that I need to take a little jaunt to Target to peruse the bathroom trash can selection for this season, which necessitates buying new rugs and a toothbrush holder, and now I am in need of some caffeine—so I stop by Starbucks, where I see a friend and strike up an hour-long conversation about the results of her recent MRI, which puts me in traffic on the way home, which makes dinner later than I had planned, so now we order pizza—and who can have pizza without a video rental? So I stop in at Blockbuster, pick up the pizza and take it home, watch the movie, feel sleepy, and go upstairs to discover that my closet light is still on from seven hours ago.

And is there a woman alive who doesn't love "Chocolate for the Feet" (shoes!)? I love to shoe shop, and my bills tell the tale. There are no raised numbers left on my American Express, and every so often I get a little "thank-you" note from the Federal Reserve. I tell John that it isn't that I overspend, it's just that he underdeposits.

A great pair of shoes can immediately improve your mood

and make you walk a little sassier. A great pair of shoes that look great *and* feel good is better than a triple score in Scrabble.

There is nothing worse than trying on a pair of great-looking shoes only to discover they are impossibly uncomfortable. In that moment, you are forced to decide between your looks and your sanity. Any woman who has spent any amount of time in a pair of killer (feeling) shoes will tell you that if she found out she had only six months to live, she would wear her most uncomfortable shoes. That would ensure that the time felt like six years. I have found that it helps to divide your closet into shoe quadrants and categorize them according to how long you know you can stay in them. There are "all day shoes" and there are "half the day shoes" and there are "one hour is my limit shoes."

I believe that great-looking/bad-feeling shoes are responsible for much of the crabbiness rampant in the female population. Maybe we shouldn't assume a female friend is crabby for no apparent reason. It could be that she is wearing the wrong size shoe — or bra. I read a statistic that claimed that between 40 to 55 percent of the adult female population is wearing the wrong size bra. Can you imagine? Why do we allow this to go on?

Let's begin a nationwide movement called the SSCC ("Shoe Survey and Chest Check") of looking to see what a crabby woman has pinching her toes and chest before we pass hasty judgment on her mood.

chemically
dependent

Have you ever gone to bed with a Crest Whitestrip on your teeth and accidentally fallen asleep with it in your mouth? And then woken up the next morning and thought, *I wonder where that thing went*, and actually been relieved when you found it on your sock?

Some products are just too weird for words. I saw a commercial the other day for a new product, and I had to go to the drugstore to see if it were for real. This new product is put out by the name we have all come to know and trust: Secret Antiperspirant. This brand has been around for years, and I have been using it since I was a teenager. The new version I saw advertised is called "Secret with Berry Sparkles." Can you believe that? Which product development specialist was two espressos over the limit *that* day? I don't know about you, but when I'm feeling a little nubby and stubbly in my armpit region, that is precisely what I want to do: make it smell like a bowl of berries and highlight it with some sparkles. Give me a break.

If you want to know where a chunk of our gross national

product is generated, you shouldn't look in the normal catego-
ries of "New Housing" or "Orders for Goods and Services." Try
looking under the category of "Chemicals" instead. I can't be the
only chick on my block with a bathroom that is overstocked with
bottles full of promises.

Our fascination with cosmetics starts pretty early, doesn't it?
I recall watching my mom put on her lipstick and not being able
to wait until I was old enough to get my own tube of that magic.
I didn't actually have my own until I was in sixth grade, and even
then I was only allowed to use the light pink (sparingly). My daughter was into my lipstick by the time she was two. I imagine that my
future grandchild will have her own tube in the neonatal unit.

Department stores really know how to rope a girl into a purchase,
don't they? They use the two words that are kryptonite to anyone
with estrogen coursing through her veins: free gift. They know that
any red-blooded American woman cannot resist the offer of free
stuff with a teensy-weensy purchase minimum of only twenty-one
dollars. Problem is, the cosmetics counter offers nothing that costs
exactly twenty-one dollars. So if you came to get the "free gift" and
you only want to purchase a tube of mascara (which is eighteen dollars for something you could get for six bucks at Walgreens), you are
then forced to purchase the incredibly overpriced pencil sharpener
for five bucks in order to get your "free gift." And we do it! Why?
Because The Two Words cause us to lose brain function.

How many "free gifts" have I purchased during my lifetime?
Possibly a hundred. How many "free gift" lipsticks were anywhere
near my shade? Possibly three. How many "free gift" eye shadows

got tossed in the trash after two years of nonuse? Probably fifty. How many bottles of free eye-makeup remover never got uncapped? At least twenty-five. That means that of my "free gift" items, I ended up actually using approximately 25 percent of the gifts. (There was one makeup line that gave away a stick of French bread with their "free gift." I used 100 percent of that one.)

Now the cosmetics companies are making you *pay* for the stuff you don't need. They call it "purchase with purchase." And haven't they made it almost impossible to determine what it is you really *need* to buy? I believe that having options is wonderful, but having unlimited options just makes us crazy. Used to be that our only concern when purchasing a foundation was that it matched our skin tone and didn't make our face break out. Now you have to determine if you need oil-absorbing, light-diffusing, anti-aging, copper-infused, pigment-matching, line-correcting, wrinkle-reducing, pore-minimizing, sheer, matte, cream, liquid, or powder. Good grief! And what is with the "all day" line of makeup? Should they even be talking about that? Have you ever heard a woman sidle up to a makeup counter and say, "I'd like something that stays on for only about four hours, please"?

When I was in third grade, there was a group of girls that sat in my desk area, and we had a little cosmetics factory going on back there. We would take our Elmer's glue and drop ten beads of it into the groove that ran down the middle of our wooden ruler. Then we would carefully slide it into the storage part under the seat of the desk as we were leaving to get on the bus in the afternoon. The glue would spread out and dry overnight, and when we arrived at our desks the next morning, voila! Fake fingernails! We would carefully peel each one out, lick the concave part, affix it to our nail, and let it dry for a minute. We were *tres chic*! They never lasted past our time on the playground, but we were stylin' for a while.

Now I have "solar tips" for my nails. It sounds as if they may be sun-powered, but it's just a fancy way to say "two-toned fakes." I go to a little nail shop a couple of miles from my house where none of the girls speaks English. We spend the hour gesturing to one another about nail length and the shape of the tip as we huff stuff that probably shouldn't be inhaled in a small space. I can't help but wonder if they are discussing my outfit or unruly eyebrows in Korean. My nail girl affixes a fake base to my nail with Super Glue (so *that's* what we should have been using in third grade!), applies a white dab of goo to the part that should be white, and applies a pink dab of goo to the part that should be pink. This is so that even *I* cannot mess it up by chipping off the paint (because it goes all the way down). I must get these special nails "filled" every three weeks or it's easy to see exactly where they are growing out. Life was easier in third grade.

The most common area of chemical dependence is found in that consistent root of discontent: our hair. The chemicals I submit myself to in the quest to enhance, get rid of, color, perm, straighten, and condition this stuff is a lab experiment all its own.

The stinkiest hair products have got to be any sort of perm, and Nair. In fact, they smell remarkably similar. Do you think that Nair is just a souped-up version of a perm that makes your leg hair super-curl until it falls off? And can anything that smells that bad be good for you?

I recall a time in my life when I vowed I would never, ever put any sort of color on my hair. I would remain a purist in this area. That was until my radiant mane turned forty and decided it would become a less-than-radiant shade of mousy brown. Having seen pictorial proof that I had entered into the "Steel Magnolias Helmet Head Society," I let my hairdresser "foil" me.

For the uninitiated, foiling is a process whereby they take the kitchen material heretofore reserved for turkey roasting and baked potatoes, cut it into little squares, paint certain areas of your hair with color, and then wrap it in foil squares to keep it from touching the parts of your hair that they aren't foiling. This takes hours. During this time, the hairdresser may make you hold your own foil squares like some sort of surgical assistant. If she asks you to do so, do not turn her down. You don't want to risk incurring the wrath of someone who could take a picture of you in this "Tina-Turner-does-Spaceman-head" state and publish it on the Internet. There is the interesting side benefit that if you get enough foil on your head and your fillings are mercury, you can pick up radio stations from Poland.

The Foil Years were good for a while. I eventually got bored with that and wanted a bigger hit (that's why it's called "chemical dependence"). When I started asking my hairdresser to consider some pink chunks, she politely told me that the foil had penetrated my brain. So I did what any reasonable woman would do: I changed hairdressers.

Trauma! Drama! Changing hairdressers is worse than breaking up with a guy! It takes longer, too. I had been trusting my head to

this woman for six years. I debated about this decision for much longer than I ever took to break up with a boyfriend. I kept prolonging
the inevitable, but it's just so hard to level with her and say, "Really,
it's not you. It's me. You won't be doing my hair, but we can still
be friends, right?" Whenever we would get up to the counter and
she would get her appointment book out and start flipping through
the pages for a date in six weeks, I simply did not have the heart to
tell her that because she wouldn't go "all the way" with the pink
chunks, I was just going to have to find someone else — so I took the
weenie route and cancelled the appointment at a later date. I never
rescheduled. I never told her why. I admit it: me equals weenie.

My new hair chick talked me into an allover color job. This
was a whole new step beyond the foil level. So I did it. Jury's out
on that one, but, after all, it's just hair. And it's a girl's prerogative
to change her mind — every six weeks.

What, then, of this chemical dependency? Do we want someone to have the courage to intervene, kidnap us in the middle of
the night, and transport us to a safe house in Arizona where we
would let our roots recur and our eyebrows and leg hair grow free?
Perhaps recite our own Two Steps to Recovery?

1. I realize that I am powerless to stop coloring my face/hair/
   nails.
2. Drive me to the nearest cosmetics department, and no
   one will get hurt.

minor
adjustments

I am going to tell you the truth. No one wants to admit that this is the truth, but it is. You might think that as you get older and as your children reach a certain age of greater independence that you will spend your time accomplishing great feats that you never had time to do because you were chasing toddlers or establishing yourself in your career. You picture yourself pursuing world peace and the total eradication of childhood disease — or just the clutter in your closet.

The ugly truth is this: you will spend most of the rest of your life making minor adjustments. Not the chiropractic kind. Not the car tune-up kind. I am talking about the ones that make you look like you are fidgety, when in reality you are 24/7 moving stuff back to where it needs to be. Your body now stands as proof that Sir Isaac Newton was right on the money.

When I was young (between the ages of fourteen and thirty, a nice long run, if you ask me), I had nice, plump, well-defined lips. They were the color that lips should be (pink), and all they needed was a little swipe of lip gloss (mmmm, remember Bonne Bell strawberry roll-on?). I was fine-looking *and* aromatherapeutic simultaneously. And did I appreciate this? This wonderland where there were invisible collagen fences that kept my lip gloss wherever I placed it? No feathering, no color running off my lips and onto my chin? Did I have any idea there would come a day when all lip fences would fall and the lip products would end up sliding off like warm Cheez Whiz off a celery stick? No, I did not. But I do now. I am painfully aware of it as I ponder why the lipstick will stick on my coffee cup through three full wash cycles but not on my lips.

I also recall a time when my body was something akin to art sculpture: firm, shapely, pleasant to behold. Now it is more like a cushy sofa, with moveable pillow cushions. I spend at least five minutes each night moving them around to the most comfortable position to sleep. I feel happy if I can just keep everything in the same zip code for the night.

There was also a time in my not too ancient history when I would look at older ladies in the mall and sniff to myself, "Don't they own a full-length mirror? Can they not *see* that their pants are riding higher and higher in the waist, resulting in the appearance of too much sock?" I secretly vowed never to join their ranks. Little did I know that this is an inevitable part of the aging process, my friends. Allow me to explain how this happens to the unsuspecting woman.

As we mature, a strange thickening of the waist area occurs. I believe that this is simply the result of all the wisdom we have acquired through our years of experience. This wisdom must reside in us some-where, so it takes up residence near our waist, as it wants to be cen-trally located. This expanding "wisdom waist" means that our pant waists are now searching, searching, searching for the smallest part of our body where they may come to rest. Unfortunately, that place eventually ends up being somewhere underneath the bottom of our bra. So you see how the Capri pants craze was born.

Unfortunately, our pantyhose are also searching, searching, searching for this smaller place to rest. They will invariably choose to search by rolling themselves downward to find their resting place. At some point between where our waist used to be and our knees, the rising of the pants will collide with the rolling motion of the pantyhose. We will be the victims of a female physics phe-nomenon known as the Clash of the Opposing Forces. Our rolling region in the middle is now totally unprotected by the smoothing power of spandex. It is our destiny. Do not fight it, Luke. Give in to the dork side.

I have come to accept the fact that my window of opportunity for everything to be working simultaneously (read: "look good") is pretty narrow. Do the math: There are a full nine days when our hair roots are showing, eight when the manicure is chipping, seven with unruly eyebrows, and five when you are just a hormonal train wreck. We end up having it all together maybe one day a month. And you can bet that is the day *no one* will see you, and it's never on the day you get your new driver's license photo taken.

I have also decided that women are better able than men to deal with the twists and turns that life throws at us because we have had to deal with hair grief over and over throughout our life-time. Elisabeth Kubler-Ross (in her seminal work *On Death and Dying*) identified the five distinct stages of grief: shock and denial, anger, bargaining, depression, and acceptance. Every woman goes through this each time she goes to the salon. First, you hand the stylist the picture of your desired hairstyle and ask if she can make this happen on your head. After vague assurances, she takes your beauty future in her hands. Thirty-eight minutes go by, and she turns you around in the chair to face the mirror. Shock! You most certainly do *not* look like the photo. Then comes denial.

"It's not that bad," you tell yourself. "When I get home and style it myself, it will be better."

That is definitely denial talking, because when you get home, ain't nobody gonna be swirling around your head with the magic products.

Then comes anger — as you are writing the check.

On the way home, you move into the bargaining stage: "Dear Lord, if you will just not let anyone see me for the next four weeks while this grows out, I will be a better person. I promise!"

Next you slip into depression. Your friends try to cheer you up with insincere, ambiguous compliments like, "It looks really . . . different" or "You're so brave!" But no amount of praying or chocolate or retail therapy can undo a bad hair episode.

Finally, you accept it. What choice do you have? In five weeks you'll have to do it all again.

Of course, some experiences are pure grief from the get-go.

I had my first mammogram a few years ago. They wanted a

baseline to compare later ones against. This was one of those experiences where they did not give me quite enough info. They just told me to go get one. No prep. Nada.

So I took my little paper with my mammogram order written on it, called the mammography unit at the local hospital, and scheduled my appointment. The day I was going in to have my baseline, I read the instruction page, which said that I was not supposed to wear any antiperspirant. I know there is a good reason for this directive, but it seems particularly cruel that on the very day you will need extra protection, you can't have it. You are going to be exposed *and* you very well may stink, too.

When I got to the mammography unit and signed in, I was very encouraged because the countertop was pink, the walls were pink, the carpet was pink, the furniture was pink, the clipboard was pink, and even the pen was pink. How bad could the whole ordeal possibly be? It looked like a Mary Kay party waiting to happen!

Upon entry, I was escorted to a changing room, where the nice lady asked me to strip down to the waist and put on The Top. If up until now you haven't had any experience with The Top, it is not immediately apparent which part goes where. It has two slits, two holes, two ties, and no instructions. I've been to college, I've graduated, so I thought that I could reason my way through this situation. I reasoned that if I were going to create a top that was specifically for this test, I would make it so that the "test subjects" would be available through the holes of The Top.

When I tried to put The Top on in this logical manner, it did not fit too well. Fortunately, I had the good sense to peek out into the hall to see how others had their tops tied on before I sashayed myself out to my certain humiliation. After quickly repositioning The Top to conform to the norm, I walked down the hall and joined the eight other women in the waiting room. It occurred to me that no matter what age or weight, each woman in that room was seated in the exact same position: with her arms crossed and supporting her unsupported "test subjects." This was also, I believe, to ward off the breeze now blowing through all the slits and holes in The Top.

One by one, we were called and walked into a room that was roughly the temperature of a meat locker. (Having listened to many a girl's story about her mammogram, I have come to the conclusion that this frigid temperature setting is obviously a part of The Mammography Unit Handbook.) Then the mammographer instructed me to remove The Top and sidle up to the massive machine in the center of the room, where I was asked to lay my "offering" upon the "altar."

Now, some of us have a greater offering than others. Others of us have just the "widow's mite." No matter what the size of your offering, they *will* reposition it. At this point, you will find that you will get very interested in the ceiling tile (just to avoid making any kind of eye contact with the technician). Whenever she has the "offering" in just the right spot, she will walk over to the other side of the room and hit a switch and down, down, down from the ceiling will descend a clear plastic Plexiglass plate. When the plate reaches a level even with your nose, you suddenly realize that this thing is going to make contact sometime soon. That is when the beads of perspiration start popping out above your lip and you are certain that it was a mistake to follow the prep sheet and skip the deodorant.

As the plate continues its descent, it does eventually make contact. This is the interesting part because it is see-through and you can watch, as though it were an out-of-body experience. Baby, it starts spreading out and s-p-r-e-a-d-i-n-g o-u-t. And for some of the "greater offering" girls, it's like too much waffle mix in the waffle iron and it starts heading over the edge. When it gets to the point that a tear is forming in the corner of your eye, the technician will shut that baby down and walk over to you and ask, "Is that all right?" And as much as you feel like screaming, "No!" you will politely murmur, "uh huh," at which point she will take the little knob on the top and torque it two more turns, which will send that little tear formation down your cheek. Then she will say the most ridiculous thing to you: "Now, be still and don't breathe." As if I could breathe when my "test subject" is squished like a pancake! And "be still"—is she crazy? Like I would attempt to pull it out of the vice grip and go for a latte right now? No way. She has *all* the power and I'm going to do *anything* she says that will hasten the liberation of my bodacious ta-ta.

In all fairness, I need to say that these technicians are only doing (a) what they have been trained to do, and (b) what is good for us (however unnatural it may seem). And I must say that in comparison to childbirth, a mammogram is a skate in the park. My mom would beg to differ after her experience last year.

She went in for her yearly mammogram and got a newbie techie. Seems the little darlin' had just graduated from mammography school and thought she saw a shadow on my mom's routine mammogram. So she called her back for a second one—and a third and a fourth. Five in all. My mom was quite a jangle of nerves afterward, although the "shadow" turned out to be nothing at all. Now, I am all for thoroughness on the job, but if I were you, I might ask my techie how many she has done. If the number is less than 750, you might want to reschedule for another day.

I have decided that the point of the mammogram is not to look for the lumps but to squish them out before they get good and started. I have also found that if you schedule your appointment on the same day as a friend, you will have much to laugh about immediately afterward. And if you and your friend go out for coffee and chocolate, them squished ta-tas will just fluff right back up.

Remember to always look your best during any medical tests because it's not what you go through in life but how you look *while* you're going through it.

hook a
sistah up!

C offee cups, greeting cards, sappy stuff. You know this one: "Friends are the chocolate chips in the cookies of life." That happens to be one that makes me want to stick my finger in the general area of my throat as I gag from cutesy-saccharine overdose. You and I both know that is *not* how it is. Friends are not the chocolate chips. If they are wonderful lifelong friends who know entirely too much about you, they pretty much are the cookie itself.

I have been blessed to have such friends in my life.

If you are of the female persuasion, you are in possession of one of life's sweetest truths: friendship is like air and water; it's essential to the soul.

For guys, I'm not sure that it is so much so. They seem to love to *do things* with each other. They like to have projects and goals and stuff to produce sweat and grime about, but they don't have the same emotion-cleansing, total-sharing needs that we chicks have. That's why it is essential to our well-being to have girlfriends.

It is key to a happy marriage, I tell ya. If you are expecting your husband to give you the kind of empathetic/sympathetic, active-listening, chocolate-sharing, soul-baring experience that you can only achieve while inadvertently sniffing a shared nail polish bottle, you are barking up the wrong tree, Fifi.

Men, for the most part, do not possess ovaries or estrogen and cannot, for the most part, intuit their way out of a paper bag. They are *not* your girlfriend and do *not* appreciate the details. If you are telling your man many details about stuff he really doesn't want to know about, you are just annoying him. I don't care how sensitive and loving he is: if he got very honest and knew that it wouldn't come back to bite him, he would admit that it is annoying on some level. I have a great husband, who is left-handed (which means that he processes things on the girlie side of his brain), and even *he* would rather I talk things out with my friends before I talk with him. Guys want to go somewhere alone (ever notice that workbenches in their workshops are built to accommodate only one?) and formulate their thoughts inside their heads and then come back and make a pronouncement of their position.

Most women, on the other hand, love to think out loud. This is what "girl talk" is all about. We want to process the information out in the atmosphere as we are forming our opinions. We never really know what it is we think until we hear ourselves say it. This is why we need girlfriends—good girlfriends. People who know an awful lot about us and continue to choose to love us in spite of it. I call these sorts of friends The Gravity and Helium Group. They give me gravity because they know my faults, my weaknesses, my issues, my stubbornness, and my weirdness. The fact that they possess this sort of knowledge keeps me grounded. If I ever start believing I'm all of that plus a bag of chips, they can gently remind me of the times I might have been more like the chip crumbs. These are the people who can do this in love and not crush me into chip dust.

These are also the people who can take my flagging balloon and fill it up with encouragement to remind me that I have flown before, I was born to fly, and I will fly again. There is nothing like the encouragement of a true friend.

When I was in high school, I was neither popular enough nor athletic enough to ever entertain the idea of being a cheerleader. There was a set of skills that divided the world into two camps: those who could be cheerleaders, and those who most definitely could not. To the rest of us, the cheerleaders were almost another class of human beings. They were tall, athletic, popular, seemingly interested in sports (or at least the guys who took part in the sports), and almost always in the Beta Club (read: smart, too). How did they do it all and look so great in those really short skirts at the same time? It was a mystery to my posse and me.

Of the two camps of the girl population (normal girls and cheerleaders), the normal girls were divided into two distinct groups: those who wanted to be cheerleaders, and those who accepted the fact that this was never *ever* going to be a possibility. I was in the latter category, and we did what we could to make ourselves feel better about not being one of the Elite Supergirls Squad: we made fun of them. And we made fun of their lame cheers, and the fact that most of the time they didn't really know what was going on with the game (usually one cheerleader *did* actually know, and she would clue the others in — this is how they knew which one should be the head cheerleader), and how they could never be separated from their pom-poms. (You never know when those could come in handy for a real emergency situation.) And why do they say, "Ready? Okay!" every single time they start a cheer? Does it really require that amount of preparation to recite rhymes and jump around?

Anyhow, when my husband and I were at our first church (while my husband was in seminary), we were invited out to a junior high football game with the head deacon and his wife. They weren't too much older than we were, and we paired off by gender once we arrived at the game. John and David went down by the fence area to stand and discuss manly stuff near the action. Robin and I sat up on the bleachers and began talking about all the stuff girls talk about. In a few minutes, the cheerleaders came out and I felt this might be my time to accomplish some major girl bonding with my new friend.

I started in on my "I just don't get the whole cheerleader thing," which had worked wonders in prior friendships. Robin nodded in agreement a couple of times but never really chimed in. As I am not the most sensitive of creatures, it took me a full three minutes of my commentary to notice that she wasn't really getting into the subject matter. It was only then that I figured out that she might have been a former cheerleader. Oh man! Why hadn't I spotted the obvious clues? She was in great shape despite having given birth twice. She had perfect hair that was always clean and bouncy. She was popular at church. She had married a football player. The weave on her carpet always ran the same direction after she vacuumed it. How did I miss it?

As I stumbled over an apology of sorts, I found out another thing about cheerleaders: some of them have a great sense of humor and a gracious spirit. Robin not only laughed about it in the moment but also continues to laugh about it twenty years later (we're still friends). Come to think of it, Robin is my only former cheerleader friend. I think the cheerleaders all stick together through life and may not befriend the lesser mortals as a rule.

I believe that the truest test of friendship is "historical shorthand" — that is, how much you *don't* have to say in order to get an idea across. This takes an extensive bank of shared experiences built up over time so that when you need to convey a whole set of emotions or perspective, you can call up a shared experience in one or two words that says it all. My best friend, Kim, and I have so many of these that it's almost unnecessary to speak in complete sentences (good thing, because we rarely do). If we want to communicate the idea of something perfectly artistic, one of us just has to reference the words "Hyperion latte," and the other sees the perfect little fern-shaped leaf the barista makes in the froth at that particular coffee establishment. It means something to us but would not translate to anyone else.

Kim and I belong to a group of friends we call the Beach Girls. There are six of us (with an occasional drifter seventh) who meet at least once a year at the beach for our mutual therapy. I am glad that somebody in our circle had some real-estate vision. The first one to get the bug for some beachfront property was Jean. She and her husband (Charles, a suave auctioneer) purchased a condo in Virginia Beach a few years back.

I must digress to tell the story of my *very slow* warm-up to the idea of beaches in general. I never have been much of a fan of the sun and sand. I think it's one of those categorical things that divides the world into two groups: cat lovers versus cat haters, city folk versus country folk, cheerleaders versus those who make fun of cheerleaders, and beach people versus mountain people. I always considered myself in the mountain category, although I only got to visit the mountains on a few vacations to Santa Fe, New Mexico, before my grandparents moved to Mississippi. But in my heart, I knew I was a mountain lover.

The only times I had been to a beach prior to my honeymoon had been to Biloxi, Mississippi, on July Fourth for the fireworks. So when my husband decided to take me to the beach for our honeymoon (nearby and cheap), suffice it to say that the beach's reputation had been inked in the "negative" column in my mind. It might have something to do with the fact that I am very fair-skinned and burn easily, or that I feel that my skin can't breathe when it is slathered with sunscreen, or that I can't abide the feeling of sand sticking to sunscreen anywhere on my body. But that was all before Virginia Beach.

When Jean first invited us to the condo, it took quite a bit of cajoling to get us there the first time. But when Jean suggested that we have a "girls only" weekend, I was *in*. No bras, no limit on chocolate or inane chatter, no subject off limits, no laundry, no responsibility. In short, no guys. No matter where a "girls only" weekend takes place, I am there. The great thing about Jean's condo is that it is on the seventh floor and the balcony faces the ocean. It is possible to spend four days at the condo, spend much time outdoors (on the balcony), and never, ever have sand anywhere on you. So were born our Beach Therapy Weekends.

We are a diverse lot, us girls. Fabulous Jean, in her late fifties, is a consummate businesswoman who, with her husband and family, built a successful business from the ground up. She has two grown children and three beautiful grandbabies.

Vivacious Ginny is an exec with IBM who just passed the fifty mark, is not married but is deeply attached to her family (sister, nieces, and nephews), and recently went through the deaths of her mom and dad, barely a year apart. She also succumbed to the call of the sea and has recently completed construction on her own piece of sandy retreat in Duck, North Carolina. She has named the home "Breath of Heaven." We all just call it "The Big House," because it is. It also helps us differentiate which seaside place we're talking about going to since we now have options. We lovingly refer to Jean's place as "The Leetle Condo," although it's only little compared to "The Big House."

Sweethearted Helen is slightly older (with all of the health problems that entails) and loves, loves, LOVES to rock the babies in the church nursery. She and her husband, Jimmy, have seen many rough times and have survived to tell the tale.

My mom, now in her early sixties, is a Beach Girl. She makes sure that we have the freshest coffee at all times and keeps everyone on track telling their stories. Ever since Dad passed away several years ago, our times at the beach have become a marker in her life, too. They allow her to mark her healing as she moves on in her life.

Recovering prepster and recent Internet mogul Kim is my best friend, and she rounds out our Beach Girls. Not really "rounds" out, as she is the littlest (she's short, okay?). We are like Mutt and Jeff. The fact that we ever got past our differences to entertain the thought of becoming friends is a story in itself.

Kim and I were a part of the same church in the same town for seven years. We had passing knowledge of each other, but she was a career girl without kids (she worked in risk management at the hospital, wore Ann Taylor suits with purely prep/professional haircuts and glasses). In contrast, I was a bona fide mom with three kids under the age of seven, long Victorian hair, country jumpers, and doily-adorned socks.

Not surprisingly, we both discounted each other as "friend material" for five of the seven years, until Kim quit her job to pursue pregnancy (her doctor advised that the workplace stress was negatively impacting her chances) and we wound up in the same Bible-study group. We decided to "friend date" each other, all the while believing it would fall apart quicker than toilet paper in a rainstorm. After all, what did we have in common?

I'll tell you what—one of the most bonding traits known to womankind: a similar, bizarre sense of humor, and a profound love of a great cup of coffee, plus the belief that chocolate is a divine gift. It is our belief that chocolate is the correct choice for when you are sad, when you are happy, when you are in love, and when you are going through a crisis. It is truly the all-occasion mood food. It also fits into the four mood groups we eat from: Elation, Ovulation, Depression, and PMSsion. When you think of a woman's brain, try to envision a chocolate truffle center. Kim has sent me chocolates on the worst days of my life—and she supersized them. Need I say more?

There are Friend Group Theories. Among our group, the theory is that there is a set group weight, meaning that we may individually lose or gain weight, but as a group, our weight will remain the same no matter what we do. So far, it's true. Be careful if you go on a diet because someone else in your group of friends will be picking up your lost pounds.

I am so thankful for my Beach Therapy Weekends. And we do tell our stories at the beach. In great emotional detail, we synopsize everything that has happened since we were last together, and then we all dish on it for hours, giving sympathy, perspective, ideas, and prayer. Sometimes we administer chocolate therapy, too. We eat after our exhausting sessions to regain strength for the next person's turn. It's much better than any brand of store-bought therapy and has turned us into the Beach Girl Mafia (meaning we know too much about each other to ever be allowed to leave the organization). And so I wrote this song for my Beach Girl Babes. (Okay, so sometimes I'm a literalist.)

You Know Too Much

I remember the day when your friendship came my way
I knew then that I'd found a friend so true

Through the weeks, months, and years—through laughter and tears
We've shared our deepest feelings as friends are wont to do
We've repeated our stories of failures and glories
We've told the honest truth about our hopes and dreams
Now we've come to the point where our lives are conjoined
And it's time to tell the truth, strange as it may seem

We'll always be friends because you know too much about me
You're far too informed to ever stray away without me
You've seen me good, bad, happy, sad, strong, and weak
You know my faults, my opinions, and my stubborn streak
We've divulged so many secrets over coffee cups
Now we're in this forever like the Mafia
We've been rowdy, pouty, let it all hang out-y
We'll always be friends because you know too much about me

You're in so many photos now that I don't have the time to cut you out
You've helped me fish my checkbook out of the garbage
If I ever made you mad, you could really trash me bad
Besides, half my stuff is stored in your garage
You've seen me in the sunshine, you've seen me through the dark times
You check my teeth to see if broccoli's stuck in there
You know which months I shave my legs, you know how much I really weigh
You know the true color of my aging hair

I hope you know I'm really only teasing ya
You're my special friend, the one I love the most
But if you ever start to get amnesia
I'll be in the clear when your memory is toast

Words and music by Anita Renfroe (Bluebonnet Hills Music/BMI)

We all need different levels of friendships in our lives to stay
on track. We need a lot of social friends. These are the kind of girls

who don't really know a lot about you but want you to come to their Tupperware parties anyway. If you can make the time in your schedule, go as much as you can. You never can tell which gathering is the one where you are gonna meet up with your potential Beach Girls!

We all need some support friends, too. These would be that group of friends with whom you share a deeper level of friendship. This may be your Bible-study group or another group of friends you meet with on a regular basis and share more about your life than what seems apparent superficially. There are two wonderful friends of mine, Stacy and Nancy, with whom I meet every other month or so for lunch at the Cheesecake Factory here in Atlanta. We have come to treasure our lunches because we all feel very safe and encouraged with each other. One fun thing we do is order according to a theme for the day (the CF menu is so large that we *have* to do that to even begin to decide what we are going to eat), and then we split the three items. One week it was an Elvis theme, another it was "Gone with the Wind" — it really doesn't matter. We just love the challenge of ordering according to a theme. Over those theme lunches, we've talked about our kids and marriages, our hopes and disappointments, our hot flashes. It's just good to share our lives with each other.

There's a deeper level of friendship that is the closest type of friend you can have. Star Jones (of ABC's *The View*) refers to this kind of friend as a "Bronco-driving friend" in reference to the now legendary scene of O.J. Simpson's white Bronco leading a police chase down the L.A. freeway. Who was driving O.J.'s Bronco? It was his longtime friend A.C. Cowlings. Now what kind of friend would show up and drive your Bronco when you are in that kind of trouble? *That's* how you know who your *real* friends are. These are the people you can call at 3:30 in the morning and they won't hang up on you. If you can count two of these in your life, you are very blessed indeed.

As important as having Bronco-driving friends is, my question to you might be, "Are *you* one to someone else?" We all want this type of friend in our life, but we must also *be* that person for someone. Friendships take reciprocity, time, effort, grace, humor, and forgiveness.

Now pack up your Bronco and get to the beach.

the hot
sign is on

I'm trying to think of *anyone* I know who is really good at "goodbyes." There just aren't too many people who relish that moment of parting or who have any feel for how to take it in stride. There's so much riding on that moment. You feel the pressure to say something memorable, something profound, something that will make the people happy when they think of you until you meet again. Something that says, "See? I'm not a complete dope."

Shakespeare and Hollywood have dreamt up some great parting scenes full of wonderful lines and touching moments. The characters always say just the right thing as the music swells and the mist rolls in. In real life, we don't get to write or memorize the dialogue ahead of time. Rather, we fumble our way through the moment and hope we don't say anything too stupid.

The other day, I got together with a girl I hadn't seen in about fifteen years, and we were discussing how Christians never really say "goodbye," because we always do that thing where we say, "If I don't see ya down here, I'll see ya in heaven." What a colossal cop-out!

Translate, "Hey, no need to bother checkin' in with you or keeping up with your life to see if you're still alive or possibly in need since we'll have all of eternity to be together." I ask you, how difficult would it be to maintain a great relationship in heaven, as we all would be in our glorified state, free from sickness, pain, and envy? Although (free from all of that), some of us will have absolutely nothing left to talk about.

But I would like to have a beautiful moment of parting with you, Gentle Reader—a moment where I say something memorable and significant, so I will talk to you about the most important spiritual matters using a metaphor so very close to my heart: the Krispy Kreme doughnut.

For those of you who live in a place where there is no Krispy Kreme shop (meaning a place where they actually *make* the dough-nuts, not just sell them off the supermarket shelf), let me first express my heartfelt sympathy and then go on to say that you have missed out on true earthly bliss and should seek one out posthaste.

Is there any other category of neon that inspires such visceral reaction as when the "Hot Now" sign is lit up at Krispy Kreme? I have yet to find it. Smelling popcorn when you walk into a movie theater is pretty potent. A whiff of the Cinnabon at the mall can entice me. But if there's red neon blazing in front of a Krispy Kreme shop, I go into Full Pavlov Response Mode. My car tires automatically know to turn in there. Fortunately for my hips, the closest doughnut shop is about twenty minutes from our house—slightly beyond the "I'll just ride up there and pick up a dozen" range.

Our family has a rule that even if we are on our way to eat a meal (with the danger of ruining our appetites) or on our way back from a meal (and are already totally full), we refuse to pass by a Krispy Kreme if the Hot Sign is illuminated. After all, it guarantees that we are nearing the Bliss Zone. When Krispy Kremes are hot off the roller, there is just nothing like them. If you've ever watched them come off the assembly line, then you've seen them get drenched in that perfect sugary glaze. Once they cool off, they are virtually undistinguishable from any other type of doughnut. But when they are hot, they are a little piece of gastronomical heaven.

When the Beach Girls were last together, Ginny showed us a new Krispy Kreme trick. If the doughnuts are more than a day old, you can slice them like a bagel and pan fry them in a little butter (flat side down). They are almost fully restored to their former hot glory, and we don't *even* want to consider what the additional butter does to the calorie tally.

But I digress.

There are people who'd like you to believe that entering into a commitment to know Christ and follow Him means you are signing up for a long list of rules and regs that will wipe out your individuality and set you on a path that leads you to the Land of the Terminally Weird. I understand how you would get that impression if you have watched much Christian TV. It seems that if you are a TV-land follower of Christ, you cannot have normal hair. There are many people preaching the gospel, singing the gospel, teaching, healing, and hosting a variety of shows on Christian TV. They seem like fairly reasonable and intelligent people (for the most part). Yet many of them sport hair colors that do not occur in nature. And if their color is in the normal range, they will most certainly have some sort of atrocious comb-over/bad rug combo or be teased Up To There. You know you've thought these same thoughts. You might have flipped right past these stations had you not been mesmerized by the hairdos going on there. Let me assure you that this is in no way reflective of the life that Christ calls us to embrace.

According to John 10:10, the verse in which Jesus gives us His personal mission statement, He says, "I came so they can have real and eternal life, more and better life than they ever dreamed of" (MSG). The life that Christ wants to give you, the one He lived, died, and came back to life again for, is sweet and full, authentic, and the difference between Kansas and Oz. He came to give life in Technicolor.

The Amplified Bible goes a step further: "I came that they may have and enjoy life." This life we are meant to enjoy has at its center a relationship with the Creator of the universe through His Son, Jesus Christ. Jesus said it was "real life," not a facsimile of it. His love covers ("glazes") our lives and brings a richness and sweetness that is the result of divine unconditional love. We were meant to live all covered in this sort of love. I'm not talking about religion; I'm talking about God all up in your stuff. Religion is like reading the menu. Relationship with God is like actually eating the meal. You could starve while reading the menu.

Ads and marketing people will tell you that you are your stuff. You are what you drive. You are what you wear. You are the number on the bottom of your bank statement.

Your conscience will tell you that you are your past. You are the sum of your choices, many of them wrong ones with difficult consequences.

Your mind will tell you that you are your fears. You are the sum of your worries about the future and if you just think about it enough, surely you can figure it out and short-circuit the impending disaster.

But Jesus said that real life is none of these things.

You are not your stuff.

You are not your past.

You are not your fears.

You are someone He loves unconditionally, someone He sacrificed His own life for, someone who matters very much to Him and to the people in your scope of influence. No matter what you have or don't have, no matter what you've done or not done, no matter what unknowns stretch out before you, you can know this: God loves you so much and He longs to make Himself at home in your life. Will you let Him?

When you experience His love and forgiveness, you will begin to understand what it means to be a person who has nothing to lose, nothing to prove, and nothing to hide. That's real freedom. That's real life.

The Hot Sign is on for you now. Come on in and taste for yourself.

ack-now-ledge-ments

Let's break that word down:

"Ack"—Latin word for "an alien exclamation of surprise"

"Now"—at the present time or moment

"Ledge"—a raised or projecting edge or molding

"Ment"—a wrong spelling of the word I meant to spell

I will now attempt to perform a feat of linguistic derring-do to prove my ability to string thoughts together that were never meant to be linked. Behold!

I am just as surprised as if an alien had landed in my very own front yard and screamed, *"Ack!"* that I am *now* a published author and, in the process, have not driven any of my friends or family to leap off a *ledge*, so now it's my turn to tell you all what you have *me(a)nt* to me. Ta-da!

Because this page in any book is normally reserved for meaningful, personal words of gratitude or shameless, flagrant sucking up (and I am nothing if not a slave to literary tradition and decorum), let's dive in, shall we?

All honor belongs to God, from whom all blessings flow, including the gift of laughter. I love Him for all the usual reasons and many that I never will be able to articulate.

One of the best reasons is my husband, John. God did a wonderful thing when He brought that man into my life. I have a hunka hunka burnin' gratitude for you, baby.

My kids (Calvin, Austin, and Elyse) are brilliant and beautiful, each one unbelievably gifted in his or her own right. I've loved them since they were zygotes and still enjoy them immensely. And I get the unqualified privilege of a front-row seat to witness all that God is doing in their lives. They make me laugh and think and pray! If I weren't their mom, I'd wish that I were.

My mom (who still lives on earth) and my dad (who is residing somewhere near the River of Life, possibly fishing) gave me everything good and strong and right and artistic in my life. They have both sacrificed so much for the cause of Christ. Their lives and love continue to bring me joy and strength. Mom, I love you. Thanks for dreaming this dream with me when you said, "Maybe you should start writing music and books instead of doing those craft shows."

JC and Vesta (John's parents) gave me John and their acceptance into their muscadine family vine (where I thereby inherited Carol and Charlie and Shelly and Sam and Joel and Kristin and Evan and CC and Scott). Thanks for letting me be me, even though it must have scared you at first.

I would also like to thank all of my Pulliam family, my Texas family (if I started listing all the relations on my mom's side, it would be its own medium-sized pamphlet—so suffice it to say, you know who you are—Hoovers, Brinkleys, Arnolds, and so on). Thank you for your love and enthusiasm and prayer for me.

Now that I have secured my spot in any and all family wills and testaments, let us move beyond to the area of "friends."

I am forever indebted to my friend Kim Carr, who is the only person (besides my mother) who will listen to every tidbit of the minutiae of my life with rapt attention. She is a gift from God, as I am overly verbal and God knew who could withstand it. For the listening, processing, praying, and holding up of cue cards while suspended from a balcony *despite your fear of heights*, you will need a neck brace to support all your eternal crowns. I will be there to push you around in the nursing home. I promise.

Special thanks to the Beach Girls (Jean, Ginny, Helen, et al, mentioned elsewhere, but they warrant another mention, just in case you were tempted to skip that chapter). "Gracias" to Juanita Angelica Caseas Blea McClung and Ruth Flanagan, who have been consistent cheerleaders for me since before I had bosoms. Also to Kay DeKalb Smith (aka "The Pioneer"), Babbie Mason, and Sue Buchanan, I owe an inordinate amount of thanks, as they have all sincerely believed in me and encouraged me when there was absolutely no reason to do so. They are faith-full encouragers.

Gobs of gratitude to my Cheesecake Factory Posse (Stacy Robinson and Nancy Burgess) for the invaluable "life lunches," where I graffitied potential chapter titles in my Palm Pilot while you guys kept right on eating *my* third of the cheesecake. I'm not bitter about it. Really. In fact, I thank you that this book is done *and* my hips are smaller. Talk about multitasking.

I'm sending out love to my personal prayer warrior, Mrs. Maizey James. I never have to wonder if she is praying for me. Blessings upon Amy Keffer-Shellem and Jennifer Skeen for that first weekend writing session in Virginia Beach. Who knew? Old-school love goes out to my college roomie Carol Stewart. For you I present "Ten Easy Ways to Get Rich Quick." I would like to give a big shout to Virelle Kidder, Carol Kent, Jennie Dimkoff, and Adelle Dickie for tirelessly attempting to hook me up with a publisher who would "get me."

Which leads me to the joy of finding Terry Behimer, editorial director at NavPress, and my editor, Traci Mullins of Eclipse Editorial Services. Terry not only "got me" but also championed this book from conception to market. Traci introduced me to the finer editorial concepts of "sequitur," "cogent," and "subject/verb agreement." This book would be utter nonsense without her skills. Now she's turned it into well-ordered, grammatically correct, sequitur nonsense.

Finally, I would like to thank Rick and Kay Warren for just being themselves. Kay has been both a friend and inspiration to me over the past several years. She has always told the truth about her life, and her transparency is a gift to the world. And to Rick, thanks for writing this century's evangelical equivalent of the Rosetta Stone, codifying the essence of what it means to follow Christ and find purpose in this life — because if you hadn't, I wouldn't have the privilege of poking a little female-driven fun at the best title in the world.

about the
author

Described as a "shot of espresso in a decaf world," the moment Anita Renfroe takes the platform, God's Spirit in her is absolutely contagious. As a comedian and musician, she enthuses with pure joy, touching the funny bone on the way to the heart. She is highly original, bodacious in her faith, and unashamedly real. Anita unleashes her spontaneous and distinctive brand of musical comedy to sold-out audiences across the United States, where the most common comment from departing attendees is, "My cheeks are hurting from laughing so much!"

As a multifaceted creative artist, her projects (comedy videos, vocal and instrumental CDs) reflect the diversity of her gifts. She makes her home in Atlanta, Georgia, with her hunk of burning love (John) and her three semi-grown children (Calvin, Austin, and Elyse). You can find out more than you ever wanted to know about her at www.anitarenfroe.com.